Elijah & Elisha

Living for God's Testimony

Titus Chu

Elijah & Elisha:
Living for God's Testimony
by Titus Chu

First Edition, 1.0: July 2005
Second Edition, 2.0: July 2014,
PDF and Print on Demand

Distributed by
The Church in Cleveland Literature Service
3150 Warren Road
Cleveland, Ohio 44111

Available for purchase online.
Printed by CreateSpace,
an Amazon.com company.

Download the PDF version of this book at
www.MinistryMessages.org

Please send correspondence by email to
TheEditors@MinistryMessages.org

Published by
Good Land Publishers
Ann Arbor, Michigan

Contents

Preface

God placed His people, the children of Israel, in the good land to be His testimony, but over time, their hearts turned away from Him. They were drawn away after idols and no longer expressed God. In order to restore His people and testimony, God raised up Elijah and Elisha. These two prophets stood for God, living for His testimony in what had become a terribly degraded situation.

We were created in God's image so that we might stand for Him here on earth and express Him in the midst of a fallen world. To do this, we must have a heart that is turned to God. In Elijah and Elisha's time, it was the worship of idols that carried people away from the living God. Today's false gods are wrapped up in the world with its "lust of the flesh and the lust of the eyes and the boastful pride of life" (1 John 2:16). In Elijah and Elisha's day, God desired to establish His testimony in the good land of Canaan. Today, the local churches are where God must have this testimony.

We are in the right place at the right time, and each of us has been equipped through creation and regeneration to live for God's testimony. We have everything we need: we are in the land, we have a spirit, and God our Savior is with us. Will we allow Him to work out His great salvation among us? Will we "prove what the will of God is, that which is good and acceptable and perfect" to an age that is lost in vanity (Rom. 12:2)? Let us prove God to our generation by giving ourselves to live for His testimony by experiencing Him in our church life today. May the Lord raise up many such prophets, and may this book be useful toward this end.

The content of this book was adapted from messages spoken by Titus Chu to college students in Montreal, Canada, in July 2004.

The Editors

God's Purpose
and Mankind's Failure

Elijah and Elisha were the greatest of God's prophets. Their experiences were profound, and their lives were meaningful. Most readers of the Bible don't expect to experience what they experienced. However, they are presented as people just like us—people who grew and developed until they became useful to God (James 5:17). If we cooperate with God to grow and develop as they did, we also shall live for God's testimony and become manifest for the fulfillment of His purpose.

Elijah—Jehovah Is God

Elijah's name is meaningful. The first part of his name, *El*, is the Hebrew word for God (Strong, no. 410). The second part, *Jah*, is a contraction for Jehovah, God's name (Strong, no. 3045). Therefore, when people spoke Elijah's name, they were saying, "Jehovah is God." In Elijah's day, many Israelites were worshiping different gods, like some people do today. Elijah's name declared, "The one true God is Jehovah!" This name matched him, for he was totally committed to God's testimony in Israel. As a prophet, he testified of Jehovah and acted according to Him. Thus he represented what it meant to be a prophet of God in the Old Testament age. In the New Testament, Elijah is mentioned more than once as the representative of all the Old Testament prophets, for he was considered the greatest among them (Matt. 11:11–14; 17:1–3; Luke 1:17).

Elisha—God Is Salvation

Elisha's name is even more wonderful than Elijah's, for his name means "God is salvation" (Davis, p. 216). Salvation is to have God with us. When the Lord Jesus Christ was born, He was called Immanuel, which literally means "God with us" (Matt. 1:23). In a good sense, Elisha's name equals the name Immanuel, because God being our salvation means that God is with us. Therefore, even though Elisha was a prophet in the Old Testament, his name implies who God becomes to us in the New Testament. In fact, everything he did prefigured how the God of grace would come to be with us so that He might become our salvation.

The Growth and Operation of Elijah and Elisha

Neither Elijah nor Elisha was born as a powerful prophet. Each of them had to go through all kinds of things before becoming useful to God. Elijah's name testified of God, but he himself was not God. Elisha's name foretold God's salvation, but he himself was not the Savior. Although they had such wonderful names, they were but human beings who had to grow and develop, each in his own way. In order to understand and be profited by them, we must understand how God worked with them and shaped them into what they became. In His work upon them, God made use of every situation and circumstance. The stories recorded in the Word are of special importance for our learning.

Eventually, both of these men operated according to God's will, plan, and economy. Elijah operated in the principle of the Old Testament while Elisha operated in the principle of the New Testament, but both lived and operated according to God's will, plan, and economy. Therefore, to understand why God raised up Elijah and Elisha, we must consider God's purpose, His work to accomplish it, and His people's failure.

God's Original Intention

At the beginning of the Bible, God said, "Let Us make man in Our image, according to Our likeness; and let them rule over the fish of the sea and over the birds of the sky and over the cattle and over all the earth, and over every creeping thing that creeps on the earth" (Gen. 1:26). The first point here is that God intended that man should bear His image and likeness, and the second is that God ordained that man should rule over the fish, the birds, the cattle, and the creeping things, even over all the earth. God set man to be the ruler over the earth and over everything related to the earth. This is what God is after—He wants man, and He wants the earth. We can never forget these two things, because God's focus is always on them.

Having God's Image and Likeness

As human beings, we must bear God's image and likeness, and we must rule over the earth. Although we certainly are human beings, we may not be so according to God's intention. If we are not bearing God's image and likeness, we may be more like cats or dogs than like God. Having God's image means we have His life inwardly, and having God's likeness means we bear His expression outwardly.

Being made in God's image is an inward matter. Since God is Spirit (John 4:24), we were made with a spirit to match Him (Zech. 12:1). Therefore, a man in God's image must be a man whose spirit is fully operating.

Our being made according to God's likeness means we bear His outward expression. Our physical bodies express God because we were made in the likeness of God. Actually, the likeness or expression of God according to which we were created is Jesus Christ. Before mankind was created, there was already a Man, for Christ as the Lamb was slain from the foundation of the world (Rev. 13:8). Jesus Christ existed as God's expression and likeness even before God created any human being, and we were created according to Him.

A Healthy Soul

We all have three parts—spirit, soul, and body (1 Thess. 5:23). These were formed when God made Adam. First He formed his body in His own likeness from the dust of the ground. Then He gave him a spirit in His own image by breathing into his nostrils the breath of life. When this happened, Adam became a living soul (Gen. 2:7).

To be what God intends for us to be, we must not only have a physical body after God's likeness but also a spirit made alive with God's own life. We also need a proper soul, for our soul is where our spirit and body come together.

The things we choose to enjoy, such as hobbies and music, should promote a healthy soul. Everyone appreciates music, but not all music produces the same result in the soul. Music can make the soul healthier, but it can also make it wilder. If we only care about enjoyment, our soul will be consumed.

Some musicians produce beautiful music, but their souls become wild and unhealthy. Because of this, they end up in immorality that damages their bodies. Some have even died at a young age from drug abuse. I feel sorry for those who get caught up in things that ruin their humanity. Healthy enjoyment, however, brings our soul into a healthy state.

Some singing only produces enjoyment and nothing else.

If this is the case, our singing may actually damage us. Our singing should produce a healthy soul that helps our spirit to be alive to God and our daily living to be proper. This is the kind of person God is after.

Anything we enjoy involves our soul. When we sing a hymn or spiritual song with a healthy soul, our spirit is put into its right place. By exercising our soul in the way God intended, we are able to enjoy His presence and sense that He is with us. Our physical body is also put into its right place, not becoming involved in improper or unhealthy behavior. Instead, we live for God's testimony.

When our soul is focused upon the Lord, our spirit will be full of life, and our daily walk in our physical body will be godly. God desires to have this kind of person. The way to be the right person for God's intention is to have a proper soul. If our soul is healthy and properly focused, nothing will hinder our spirit from being healthy, for we will not participate in anything that results in loss.

Ruling over the Earth

For His testimony, God must gain a group of people who bear His image and likeness, that is, who have healthy souls, strong spirits, and a godly living. This alone is not enough, however, for God's people must also rule over all the earth. God's testimony is produced when the right people are ruling upon the earth. God's people cannot just be up in the air, living a heavenly Christian life. They must be related to the earth, the land.

When God's people are caught by things such as money, they aren't related to the land anymore, for money isn't the land. Knowledge and education are not the land either. The apostle Paul ruled over the earth by establishing and building up local churches everywhere he went. The local churches are the land to which we must be related for the sake of God's testimony. If we wish to be proper before the Lord, our heart must desire what He desires—the church (Eph. 5:25).

It may seem difficult to labor on the land where we are. We may feel our church is weak or that it is only for a certain group in the church and not for us. When the situation in our local church seems discouraging, we may feel that the land doesn't have much value. However, rather than complain about the church being too poor, weak, old, or discouraging, we should labor to make it healthy. If we are healthy, we should be able to produce a healthy situation wherever we are.

In Taiwan, if there is even a small bit of land available, someone will work it. If the land is mountainous, they will terrace it and grow rice or vegetables. If the soil is not good for growing crops, they will turn it into a pond and raise fish. We should be like this in our church life, treasuring what has been given to us. Healthy people will produce good land, and good land will produce healthy people. God needs both man and land for His testimony.

Perhaps we feel that the land is good, but that we ourselves are poor and weak. We may think that we have no ability to produce anything of value in the church life. Yet in the same way that healthy farmers produce good land, the good land can produce healthy farmers. In the United States, many farmers feel that farming less than a thousand acres is a waste of time. What a contrast to Taiwan! But the high quality of the land in the United States produces many successful farmers. The very richness of the land can make up for the shortage and failure of those who work it until they are molded into capable and successful farmers. It is the same in the church life.

A History of Failure

After God created man in His image and likeness, Adam and Eve disobeyed God, and mankind became corrupted and fell away from God (Gen. 3). Adam's first son, Cain, became a murderer (Gen. 4). Although God provided Seth to replace the murdered Abel, mankind's condition continued to grow worse. Eventually, they degraded to the point that God could no longer tolerate it (Gen. 6). Therefore, He destroyed mankind with a flood and began again with Noah (Gen. 7–8).

God was able to save humanity through Noah because he was willing to build the ark. Thus God was able to spare eight people from His judgment. After the flood, Noah became a farmer and planted a vineyard. From the grapes of his vineyard he made wine for his own enjoyment, and one day he became so drunk that he lay naked in his tent (Gen. 9:20–21). Even a man so useful to God can fall. Those who do not know God fail, and those who know God also fail. The history of fallen mankind is a history of failure and degradation.

Man and the Land

Out of fallen mankind God eventually gained one man, Abraham, who lived before God by faith. He trusted and believed God (Gen. 15:6; Heb. 11:8–19). Through Abraham, God produced a people and eventually gained David.

From Noah to Abraham God took a big step, and from Abraham to David He took another big step. In Abraham, God gained a man, but through David, God gained a man plus the land. Regarding the land, Abraham only had God's promise, but it was David who actually established a kingdom and ruled for God on the earth (Acts 7:45–46). Now God had man with His expression ruling in the land. At least in type, God finally had His expression, His testimony, upon the earth.

Failure and Division

After David, his son Solomon reigned in his place (1 Kings

1:38–39). In Solomon, God still had a man with the land.
Under Solomon, the kingdom was even enlarged. Because
he asked God for wisdom rather than for riches or a long life,
we might say that Solomon was a spiritual man (3:5–14). He
wrote Proverbs, Ecclesiastes, and the Song of Songs. Yet Solomon also failed. The seed of corruption somehow entered
into this spiritual man. Because he married many foreign
wives, all kinds of foreign idol worship were brought into
the good land (11:1–10). During David's reign, there was
only Jehovah, but during Solomon's reign, many false gods
were brought in among God's people that drew them away
from God.

As a result of Solomon's failure, the kingdom was divided during the reign of his son Rehoboam (vv. 11–13).
Since man was no longer enjoying God properly in the
land, the expression of God's image inwardly and likeness
outwardly in the land was lost, and the kingdom became
divided. The kingdom of Judah lay in the south, retaining
Jerusalem along with its temple. In principle, the kings of
Judah were kept by God at a higher level. In the northern
kingdom of Israel, however, people no longer worshiped
God in Jerusalem, but instead worshiped golden calves set
up by Jeroboam at Dan and Bethel (12:26–33). Without
exception, every king of this northern kingdom was terrible. They went from bad to worse until Ahab, who became
the worst king of all.

A Most Evil King

King Ahab did what was evil in the sight of the Lord. He
even considered it "a trivial thing" to walk in the sins of Jeroboam by continuing the worship of the golden calves at Dan
and Bethel (1 Kings 16:31). His considering it a trivial thing
meant he did not think how he served God was important.
As the king, Ahab should have taken the lead among God's

people to bear the testimony of the Lord in the good land, but instead, he felt it was sufficient to worship the Lord in the perverted manner invented by Jeroboam. He did not give much thought to what the Lord wanted, nor did he inquire of the Lord as to how he should worship the God of Israel. Instead, he simply followed tradition.

Today, even though we may know about God's heart's desire, we likewise often take things for granted. Like Ahab, we may be content to walk according to a false situation that owes itself to tradition rather than to the living God. To follow and serve God is a sober matter, but people often take it lightly.

The land, however, still belonged to the Lord. We are told that "Ahab the son of Omri did evil in the sight of the Lord more than all who were before him" (1 Kings 16:30). The phrase "in the sight of the Lord" indicates that the land was still the Lord's. The problem was with man, not with the land.

Ahab's name did not have a wonderful meaning like Elijah's or Elisha's. Their names testified of God, while Ahab's name means "a father's brother" (Davis, p. 19). Our father's brother is someone who loves and cares for us as a relative, but doesn't pay the price to raise us. Each of us has a father who gave us life. If he is a good father, he is willing to suffer on our behalf and pay a price for us to make the most of our life. However, our father's brother merely says, "We happen to be related."

To be Ahab, a father's brother, means that we love God's land, the church life, but we are not willing to pay a price for it. We can claim a relationship with God, but we won't pay any price for the sake of His testimony. We can say we love God, but our life is not for God. The church life deteriorates when we take the attitude of father's brothers, knowing all about the church, yet not giving ourselves to it. May the Lord have mercy on us that we would not become a father's brother in our church life.

Worshiping Foreign Gods

Although Ahab as the king could have done something to bring God's people back to God, he married Jezebel, the daughter of the Sidonian king Ethbaal (1 Kings 16:31). This marriage reveals just how far his heart was from the Lord. After he married her, he was brought under the influence of her idol worship. We may think that a husband should be the one who influences his wife, but every wife has a way to influence and control her husband. Therefore, Ahab began to worship and serve her god, Baal. He even built Baal a temple in the capital city, Samaria (v. 32). Other gods had come in during Solomon's reign, but the Lord was still being worshiped; they did not totally replace the Lord. Under the reign of Ahab, however, the worship of the Lord was almost completely replaced by the worship of Baal. The people's hearts were turned aside.

The Asherah and the Curse

Not only did Ahab consider it a trivial thing to worship the golden calves and marry Jezebel, a promoter of Baal worship, but he also built the Asherah, which was another kind of idol. Asherah means "happy" (Strong, no. 842) and comes from a root word meaning "to go forward" (Strong, no. 833). This kind of idol represents mankind's desire for happiness, including the desire for progress by going forward. Once people feel they are making progress and achieving happiness, they may think they no longer have any need for God.

The eventual result of Ahab and Jezebel leading the nation of Israel into idolatry was to bring the entire country under a curse. During the reign of Ahab, a man named Hiel the Bethelite rebuilt the city of Jericho, which had been cursed by Joshua according to the word of Jehovah (Josh. 6:26; 1 Kings 16:34). Hiel laid the foundation of Jericho at the cost of his firstborn son, and he set up its gates at the cost of his youngest son. The rebuilding of Jericho characterized how the entire nation had come under God's curse. Due to the establishment of the rival worship of Baal and the Asherah and the lightness with which they regarded the worship of the Lord, the people found themselves in a cursed situation. They were wretched and full of darkness. It was in such a dark and cursed situation that God raised up Elijah and Elisha to be His prophets.

2

Elijah's Growth and Development

The Background of Elijah

In the midst of the dark and degraded situation under King Ahab, Elijah abruptly appeared on the scene, coming seemingly out of nowhere (1 Kings 17). As Ahab and his wife Jezebel were leading the people astray after Baal and the Ashcrahs, Elijah presented himself as one standing for the testimony of the Lord: "Now Elijah the Tishbite, who was of the settlers of Gilead, said to Ahab, 'As the Lord, the God of Israel lives, before whom I stand, surely there shall be neither dew nor rain these years, except by my word'" (v. 1). This bold prophecy formed the basis for Elijah's life and operation as a spiritual man.

All that the Bible tells us about Elijah's background is that he was a Tishbite from Gilead. The word "Tishbite" means "to take captive; turning back; recourse" (Potts, p. 240), so a Tishbite was one who had been taken captive. Elijah was a captive from among the inhabitants of Gilead, which means "heap of witness" (Potts, p. 95). The first occurrence of this name in the Bible is when Jacob was fleeing from Laban, his father-in-law. After Laban overtook Jacob in the hills of Gilead (Gen. 31:17–23), the two parties set up a heap of stones there and swore not to pass by the heap to harm one another. This heap became a heap of witness, for it bore the testimony of their oath.

In Elijah's day, the whole land was under the captivity of Baal and the Asherah—the pursuit of prosperity and happiness. Elijah, however, whose name means "Jehovah is God," was a captive of the Lord, and his captive life was a heap of witness, testifying to all the people that the Lord was God. These seemingly small details reveal much to us about what kind of person Elijah was. When people asked Elijah what his name was, he had to respond, "Jehovah is God!" When they asked what his nationality was, he told them, "A captive of the Lord God." If they questioned him further about where he lived, he would tell them, "A heap of testimony of the Lord God." A person who can respond like this is a spiritual man.

Bold and Crazy

The very first time the Bible mentions Elijah is when he walked up to the king himself and boldly declared that "there shall not be dew nor rain during these years, except by my word." God honored his bold word. Do we have the boldness to make this kind of declaration to those around us? I think Ahab looked at this peculiar man before him and thought, "He must be crazy." Actually, this is probably why Elijah survived. If the king had taken him seriously, he would have had him seized and put in prison until he gave the word for rain to come. Instead, he probably just thought Elijah was crazy and let him go.

All who love Jesus should be considered crazy by those around them. Everyone around us is striving to impress others, but we should say, "My name is 'Jesus is Lord.' My background is that I am a captive of Christ. My life is not given to the pursuit of worldly success or prosperity but to be a testimony to my Lord Jesus Christ." If we live this way, people will consider us crazy and won't invite us to their ungodly, worldly events, since we don't talk about anything except Jesus Christ our Lord.

When I attended Taiwan University, I was probably the only Christian in a class of 480 students. All of my classmates were extremely ambitious to achieve success and fame, yet I was simply loving the Lord. At the time, they all thought I was crazy. Recently, I talked to some of them. One told me, "We all knew that you were very...special." He meant crazy. Now that we have grown old, most have retired. They marvel that I have only grown busier. This is because my name is "Jesus is Lord." I am His captive, and I have given my life to be a heap of witness to Him. If we give ourselves to live this kind of life, others won't be able to figure us out.

No Dew or Rain

Elijah prophesied that there would be no dew or rain in the land except by his word. He spoke this prophecy in the God-chosen and God-blessed good land where God's people dwelt. This land was blessed with dew and rain, causing it to be wonderfully fertile. Yet Elijah swore that both this dew and this rain would be dried up.

Dew has four meanings in the Bible. First, dew represents the source of blessings. Isaac blessed Jacob with the dew of heaven, the fatness of the earth, and an abundance of grain and new wine (Gen. 27:28). With the dew comes the abundance of grain and new wine, but when the dew is dried up, there is no way for the land to yield its fatness. This is why, if we enjoy the Lord as the dew in the morning, we will be blessed all day long. Second, dew stands for the heavenly things. Moses blessed the tribes of Joseph in this way: "Blessed of the Lord be his land, with the choice things of heaven, with the dew, and from the deep lying beneath" (Deut. 33:13). This verse reveals that dew is one of the choicest things of heaven. Third, dew signifies the blessing of life. There was dew in the place where "the Lord commanded the blessing—life forever" (Psa. 133:3). Fourth, dew denotes spreading and propagation.

Concerning the Lord, David wrote, "From the womb of the dawn, Your youth are to You as the dew" (Psa. 110:3). Since dew is what comes forth from the womb, it represents the propagation of life. These aspects of dew go together. The blessings we receive are heavenly, not earthly; the more we enjoy the heavenly blessings, the more blessing of life we enjoy; and, through such heavenly, life-giving blessings, God's life spreads and is propagated.

Rain is also significant in the Bible. Moses told the children of Israel that if they loved and obeyed the Lord, "He will give the rain for your land in its season, the early and late rain, that you may gather in your grain and your new wine and your oil" (Deut. 11:14). Rain is the source of a rich harvest, causing the land to bring forth every variety of produce. Rain also signifies God and man working together so that something may be produced. According to Genesis 2:5, no rain fell until a man was present to till the earth, meaning that rain comes when we cooperate with God.

All of this shows how significant Elijah's word to King Ahab was. Without dew, all the blessings of the land would dry up. There would be no heavenly things to enjoy, no blessing of life, and no propagation. Without rain, there would be no harvest, because Israel was not willing to work together with God. To have no dew and no rain means that the whole country would be dried up physically and spiritually. The Lord would no longer bless the land until Elijah said so, and that would not be until Ahab led the people to turn their hearts back to God.

Elijah's Need to Grow

Although Elijah spoke such a bold word to Ahab, the king didn't seem to believe what he said. Therefore, he let him go without imprisoning or killing him, giving God the opportunity to train Elijah further. In this, his first recorded act as a prophet, Elijah had done an excellent job. He must have been very happy with himself. As he left the palace, he must have even been walking tall. He probably wanted to tell everyone he passed what he had just done. No doubt, people must have begun to talk about him.

This sometimes happens when people begin to serve the church with good results. Suddenly, others start appreciating them. They say, "You are the future of the church." This was said to me when I was young, along with a few thousand others attending a conference. Yet how many from that conference are serving the Lord today? Only a very, very small number. Our success in serving the Lord can cause us to become proud, so the Lord must bring us on further through experiences that help us to grow.

Although he had been successful, Elijah was still an inexperienced prophet. He had no idea what he was doing. He also had little understanding of how the Lord operated or of what the Lord wanted to do. So right after his great success, the Lord spoke to him. Did He say, "Good work, Elijah. Let Me bless you outwardly as a reward, so that everyone can appreciate you more"? No, He told him, "Go away from here and turn eastward, and hide yourself by the brook Cherith, which is east of the Jordan" (1 Kings 17:2). It was time for Elijah to learn the real lessons so that he could grow.

Growing by Being Humbled

In order to get to the brook Cherith, Elijah had to cross the Jordan River. The Jordan is extremely significant in the Bible. Its name means "descending" (Potts, p. 144). This was the river the Israelites crossed to enter the good land. They left twelve stones in the riverbed representing the twelve tribes of Israel (Josh. 4:9). In figure, all the tribes of Israel were buried there. When the Lord sent Elijah across the Jordan, He was asking Elijah to descend, to lower himself. Elijah was too satisfied with the little victory he had with Ahab. Without this lowering, Elijah would probably have relived this glorious moment over and over the rest of his life. In order to grow, he had to descend from the heights of his pride and self-admiration.

When we first began to love the Lord and follow Him, something peculiar happened—we started thinking we were important. We believed that we were the future of our church. However, the future of the church depends on its members being freed from their feeling of "selfishness or empty conceit" by lowering themselves and descending into the death waters of the Jordan (Phil. 2:3–5).

So Elijah came to the brook Cherith, which is east of the Jordan. The name of this brook means "cutting; piercing; slaying" (Potts, p. 65). It was not enough for Elijah merely to descend. He needed also to be cut, pierced, and slain. After Elijah descended into the Jordan and came to the brook Cherith, God was cutting him to bring him lower and lower. Cut by cut, God was taking away everything Elijah could boast in.

Have we been cut by the Lord? He intends to cut away all the marvelous things we show off to others. He cuts away all our self-confidence. He doesn't cut us just once but again and again. When He cuts us even a little bit, we think we have suffered so much and pray, "Lord, I am so glad I made it through this cutting. Thank You that it's finished." Yes, we made it through that cutting, but an even bigger cutting is on its way. This is a difficult process to pass through, but it is crucial for our growth in the Lord. Although we often pray, "Lord, take it easy on me. Please don't cut me so much," we should thank Him that He is so faithful to cut away these things.

Elijah had to survive by drinking the water from that little brook and by being fed by ravens (1 Kings 17:4). This was part of the lowering and cutting process. Ravens are dirty birds that live on carrion. These birds brought meat and bread to Elijah in the same beaks that ate corpses. I don't know what kind of meat they brought to him, but I guarantee it wasn't prime rib. It was probably something peculiar, but at least Elijah could sanitize it by cooking it. When the ravens brought bread, however, he couldn't do much to clean or re-cook it. All he could do was eat it.

How long did he live in such humiliation? My guess is that it was at least a year. Eventually Elijah began to realize that he could live as a clean person amidst the uncleanness of his situation. He wasn't merely in the company of these foul, unclean ravens; every day he was fed by them.

Elijah being fed by the unclean ravens is a picture of our relationship to the worldly people around us. As we begin to love the Lord and His people, we become aware that we are living in the midst of many unclean people on every side. We are not floating three feet above the ground and overcoming every moment. We should learn to treasure the unclean coworkers, colleagues, neighbors, and relatives in our lives. Can we befriend those who are unclean? This doesn't mean we ought to do everything they do, but they should feel that they can talk to us about their problems and that we are willing to be with them, to listen to them, and to love them. We should learn to be around all kinds of people. Not only will we become a help to them, but we ourselves will also be fed by them. Remember how Jesus befriended the tax collectors and sinners (Matt. 9:10; 11:19). He didn't participate in their sins, but He was always happy to talk and eat with them. After Jesus shared the good news with the sinful woman at the well, He told His disciples, "I have food to eat that you do not know about" (John 4:32). This is what Elijah learned by being fed by the filthy ravens.

Growing by Being Refined

The lowering, cutting, and humiliation were the first stage of the Lord's training of Elijah. Then, after a period of time, even the brook dried up. This caused Elijah to suffer further, but it was a means for the Lord to bring Elijah to another level of spiritual growth.

The Christian life is interesting. Sometimes the Lord brings us down before the Jordan to the brook Cherith to cut away our pride and self-confidence. In this healthy process of growth, we become very dry. The brook Cherith dries up. It is easy to get discouraged at this point and pray, "Lord, although I did not like the lowering and cutting, I was growing in that situation. Now that the brook has dried up, what am I to do?" Actually, this dryness leads into another stage of growth.

Some things that the Lord gives us as new Christians are not meant for us to enjoy our whole lives. As we grow, these things fit us less and less. The very things that helped us grow in Christ will bring us onward to another stage, causing us to leave those things behind. As Christ causes those things to dry up, we are forced to go on further in Him. When we are ready to advance, we find that the Lord has richer blessings prepared for us.

Elijah must have become desperate when the water began to dry up. Then the word of the Lord came to him, saying, "Arise, go to Zarephath, which belongs to Sidon, and stay there; behold, I have commanded a widow there to provide for you" (1 Kings 17:9). Zarephath means "refinement" (Potts, p. 247). The Lord wanted to refine Elijah because he was still wild when he spoke to the king and when he lived by the brook, being fed by ravens. This wild person needed the Lord's refining work to become a man of God.

After bringing us low and cutting us, the Lord begins to refine us. Many new believers are quite wild in the way they love the Lord. In a sense, this is the way they are supposed to be. Even in human life this is true. Young people tend to be rough. They argue with their fathers and hurt their mothers' feelings. But once they begin to experience life and grow more, the roughness disappears, and they become finer.

Elijah was a rough hero when he appeared before the king, so God took him to Cherith to make him more humble. Although the Lord's cutting had caused him to grow and become less proud, he was still rough around the edges.

So Elijah traveled to Zarephath, to God's refinery. As he came to the entrance of the city, he met the widow the Lord had spoken of as she gathered sticks. He immediately called her to bring him some water, because he was so dry. As she was fetching the water, he asked her to bring some bread also. She told him, "As the Lord your God lives, I have no bread, only a handful of flour in the bowl and a little oil in the jar; and behold, I am gathering a few sticks that I may go in and prepare for me and my son, that we may eat it and die" (1 Kings 17:12). Elijah had a way to respond to this despairing widow. He told her, "Do not fear; go, do as you have said, but make me a little bread cake from it first and bring it out to me, and afterward you may make one for yourself and for your son. For thus says the Lord God of Israel, 'The bowl of flour shall not be exhausted, nor shall the jar of oil be empty, until the day that the Lord sends rain on the face of the earth'" (vv. 13–14).

Do you see the difference between Elijah and the widow? Elijah could say, "Thus says the Lord God of Israel." But the widow could only say, "As the Lord your God lives." Suppose there were three believers at different stages of maturity in the Lord. The youngest would say to those who were more mature, "The Lord your God." The one with some maturity should be able to say, "The Lord my God." But the most mature should be able to say, "The Lord God of Israel." Elijah and the widow both spoke of God, but they apprehended Him at two different levels. Although the widow knew that the Lord was Elijah's God, she had no understanding of how He operated. All she knew was that there was only enough food for one more meal, after which she and her son would die. But Elijah was bold to proclaim, "Thus says the Lord God of Israel," even though the Bible doesn't record that the

Lord said any such thing. Elijah simply knew the Lord, His speaking, and that He was the God of Israel. As the God of Israel, the Lord always cares for His testimony.

Daily Supply

Elijah told the widow to make a bread cake for him first, and then to make another for herself and her son. Thankfully the widow didn't say, "If I give you even a little bit of our food, that means we will live three hours less." Elijah had a way to speak to her that caused her to believe what he said. He told her that if she did as he asked, "The bowl of flour shall not be exhausted, nor shall the jar of oil be empty, until the day that the Lord sends rain on the face of the earth" (1 Kings 17:14).

This is God's way. The principle in the Bible is that God always supplies our need daily. When the children of Israel were in the wilderness, God sent manna daily according to their need (Exo. 16:4). In the New Testament, Jesus taught His disciples to pray, "Give us each day our daily bread" (Luke 11:3). In His governmental provision, God will only give us a little meal and a little oil each day. The bowl of meal will never give out, and the jar of oil will never fail.

Our way is different. If we haven't read the Bible all week, we may read twenty chapters on the weekend to make up for it. Maybe we should read twenty chapters, but this doesn't make up for the days we missed. God only provides enough meal and oil for one day at a time. He does not like to give us more than we can take in at one time. His principle is to give us His riches day by day, one portion at a time. If we skip our portion today, we cannot make up for it tomorrow. The size of the portion may vary according to our ability to receive, but the Lord will never give us less than we need, nor will He give us more than we can take in. We should tell the Lord, "Give us each day our daily bread." No matter how fervent we are, every day He will give us only that day's spiritual supply.

Perhaps our church life is discouraging. Nevertheless, even in the worst circumstances, God promises daily bread. This is the principle of God's provision.

 Suppose Elijah had told the widow, "God is going to multiply the meal and oil so that you can make as many bread cakes as you want. You could fill your whole house with bread, or you could open a bread restaurant and get rich." If God supplied us in this way, we would no longer have had to rely upon Him for our daily supply. He causes us to rely on Him every day. We cannot store up for tomorrow. We can only receive the supply He provides for us today.

Raising the Dead

 As Elijah was learning the principle of God's divine provision by eating his bread day after day, God showed him something more—the principle of His resurrection power. Sadly, the widow's son died, and in her grief, the widow lashed out at Elijah, saying, "What do I have to do with you, O man of God? You have come to me to bring my iniquity to remembrance and to put my son to death!" (1 Kings 17:18). Her words were unreasonable. After all, Elijah did not kill her son. In fact, he saved them both from starvation when he first came to them.

 Often when one person accuses another in such a way, the accused reacts in a fleshly way. Elijah could have lost his temper and said, "Are you so foolish? Your son would have died long ago if I had not come!" When we are in our flesh, we only see how people falsely accuse us. We never remember grace. No matter how much we do for people, we should not expect their gratitude. It simply isn't in human nature, unless a person is transformed of God.

 Instead of rebuking this woman, he took her son from her and brought him to the upper room. He laid the boy on his own bed and cried out, "O Lord my God, have You also brought calamity to the widow with whom I am staying, by causing her son to die?" (v. 20). Look at how refined Elijah had become. He didn't lose his temper when the widow became angry with him, and he was sensitive in his prayer. He was indicating to the Lord that he was the Lord's witness while he stayed at the widow's house. He expected the Lord to bless those around him. Since he was a guest of this widow, the Lord should bless her for His name's sake.

After Elijah prayed, he stretched himself out on the child three times and called out to the Lord, saying, "O Lord my God, I pray You, let this child's life return to him" (v. 21). The Lord listened to Elijah and restored the boy to life.

To raise the boy from the dead, Elijah first told the widow to bring her son to him. Sometimes people are unwilling to be separated from their situation of death, so it is impossible for us to help them. Had the widow clung to her dead son, Elijah would not have been able to help him.

Second, Elijah took the son from her and brought him up into the upper room. He raised him out of a low situation into something higher. To help him, Elijah had to bring him out of deadness into a situation that was alive.

Third, Elijah laid the boy on his own bed, the very place where he experienced rest. If we want to give life to those around us, we must bring them to the things that give us rest. If singing hymns is a source of strength and comfort to us, we should bring others to this to find strength and comfort as well. We can help those who are dead by bringing them into the things that cause us to have the Lord's sweet presence.

Fourth, after Elijah prayed such a sensitive prayer to the Lord, he stretched out on the boy three times. To stretch out on him means that he identified himself with the child. Good gospel preachers don't judge others, because that causes them to shrink away. Instead, they identify with those they are trying to reach. Elijah did this three times. The number three signifies resurrection, as seen when the Lord resurrected on the third day.

These four steps show the principles of resurrection life. Most of the people around us are walking corpses, dead in their trespasses and sins (Eph. 2:1). They all need to be saved and healed. To heal them, we must first help them separate themselves from their dead situation. If they will not come out of their death, it will be very difficult to help them. Then, we must bring them into the "upper room" and place them on our "bed." This is to bring them into something higher by ushering them into the Lord's presence through the very things that bring us into restfulness before the Lord. Finally, while crying out to God, we must identify with them and bring them to our own enjoyment and experience of Christ. If we are able to care for the dead ones in this way, we will bring them out of death to join us in the land of the living.

3

Elijah
and Obadiah

Standing versus Compromising

After Elijah prophesied that there would be no rain or dew in Israel until he commanded it, the Lord upheld his word. This drought caused a severe famine throughout the land. After three years, the word of the Lord came to Elijah, saying, "Go, show yourself to Ahab, and I will send rain on the face of the earth" (1 Kings 18:1).

At this same time, King Ahab sent his steward Obadiah through the land to search the springs and valleys for grass to save some of the horses and mules. He sent Obadiah through half the land, while he himself traveled through the other half (vv. 5–6). It is hard to believe that a king would care so much for mules when all his people were in danger of starving to death.

Obadiah was a good man who "feared the Lord greatly" (v. 3). When Jezebel was persecuting the Lord's prophets, "Obadiah took a hundred prophets and hid them by fifties in a cave, and provided them with bread and water" (v. 4). Both he and the prophets he hid feared the Lord, but none of them were useful to God for His testimony. There is a serious lesson to be learned from this. We may be good and God-fearing yet still completely useless to God for His testimony.

Since Obadiah's position gave him ready access to Ahab,

why didn't he warn him against following Baal and speak to him about God's ways? He should have told Ahab, "Stop your worship of Baal. It is wrong for a king of Israel to tolerate the worship of false gods, let alone to promote and establish such things. Return to the Lord and worship Him only, because He alone is God!" But apparently Obadiah and the prophets he protected said nothing. How terrible it is that though they were prophets of the Lord, not one of them dared to take a stand for God's testimony.

Any unwillingness of God's prophets to take a stand becomes a great source of weakness to the Lord's testimony. Obadiah, who had a first-class education, high-ranking job, and great worldly success, should have told the king that he would resign if the king continued his disgraceful and blasphemous behavior. Obadiah was good—his name even means "servant of the Lord" (Hitchcock)—yet he was completely passive when it came to God's testimony. Rather than actively taking a positive stand for the Lord, he went along with the situation. If we are Obadiahs, we might be able to say, "I love the Lord. I follow the Lord. I love His people and His prophets, and I take good care of them." But are we willing to give up everything and make every sacrifice, including laying down our own lives, for the sake of God's testimony? We may think that becoming an Obadiah is a good thing, but this will greatly damage us in our life-long pursuit of Christ.

Obadiah's passivity bothers me even more than Ahab's outright corruption. Certainly Ahab made a serious mistake in marrying Jezebel. He should have known better than to marry a Gentile woman, especially one who worshiped Baal. This marriage was the source of all the failures and tragedies of Ahab's reign. Yet even such an evil wife could have been balanced, or her impact mitigated, simply because Ahab had a close friend and steward named Obadiah who greatly feared the Lord. Yet Obadiah was unwilling to pay the price to uphold God's testimony.

Often the problems in the church life are not caused by the Ahabs but by the Obadiahs. Many who claim to serve the Lord are Obadiahs, for they are unable to take a clear stand for the Lord's testimony.

What was the difference between Elijah and Obadiah, or between Elijah and the one hundred prophets that Obadiah hid? After all, they were not false prophets or prophets of Baal. They were prophets of the true God and served Him. The difference was that Obadiah and the prophets were all cowards. They cared more for their own lives than for the Lord's interest. As prophets, they should have cared only for the Lord's interest and testimony. Otherwise, why be a prophet? Yet they were too fearful to tell the king that he was wrong and was leading the people astray.

Caring for the Lord's Testimony

We should appreciate the fact that Obadiah hid the Lord's prophets, but we also must realize that because Obadiah failed to take a stand, godliness disappeared in Israel. He was very good, but he was not godly. We should ask ourselves: are we merely good, or are we godly? Many Christians are quite nice. They desire to make their church elders happy, and they don't want to be rebellious. But they often forget that what God wants is a kingdom and testimony. For this, what He needs is not nice people or even good people, but captives—men and women who are completely captured by Him and are willing to pay any price for the sake of His testimony.

This is why God could use Elijah. His name implies that he was for God's testimony, and his background implies that he was captured by God. He lived only according to God and His desire, regardless the price. This was the difference between Elijah and Obadiah. Throughout the Old Testament, God used many prophets, but at this critical juncture, God could use no one but Elijah. All of the other prophets and servants of God cared about being good, but not about being godly.

Our primary concern should not be our personal Christian need but Christ's testimony. Our life-long prayer should be, "Lord, I don't want to be just a good person. I want to be godly." There is a huge difference between good and godly Christians, between being pious and taking a stand, between being religious and living out the divine life. A religious person lives in the principle of Obadiah, while a godly person lives in the principle of Elijah. A religious person does things for God, but a godly person takes care of God's testimony.

To do things for God is to try to be helpful. Obadiah certainly was being helpful to God when he saved one hundred prophets and even fed them. Yet he refused to put himself at risk to uphold the truth that the Lord is God.

We are often very much like Obadiah in our way of thinking. For example, some may feel an inner leading from the Lord to serve Him full-time. However, when they consider giving up a promising career in engineering or computer programming, they simply can't bring themselves to do it. Instead they reason, "I can work and make money to support others to serve the Lord. If I earn sixty thousand dollars a year, then every year I can offer six thousand dollars as my tithe. Over my career I will offer over two hundred thousand dollars to the Lord and His servants." This is Obadiah logic. They claim that they are rendering a service to God, but a partial consecration does not satisfy Him. I am not saying that to uphold the Lord's testimony we must all serve Him full-time, but we must be faithful if He calls us. The Lord doesn't want us merely to do things for Him. He wants us to give our entire being to Him.

Obadiah Meets Elijah

Obadiah met Elijah while passing through the countryside on King Ahab's errand. Elijah told him, "Go, say to your master, 'Behold, Elijah is here'" (1 Kings 18:8). Rather than going to Ahab, Elijah wanted Ahab to come to him. He maintained a higher position for the sake of the Lord's testimony.

Obadiah's response was timid and fearful: "What sin have I committed, that you are giving your servant into the hand of Ahab to put me to death?" (v. 9). He was afraid that, after he told Ahab that Elijah wanted to see him, Elijah would disappear and Obadiah would be executed by the angry king. After spending years in seclusion at the brook Cherith and in Zarephath, Elijah had acquired a reputation for disappearing. Obadiah's fearfulness threatened the dignity of God's prophet, because he wanted to escort him personally into the king's presence rather than allow Elijah to wait for the king. Eventually, Elijah was forced to swear, "As the Lord of hosts lives, before whom I stand, I will surely show myself to him today" (v. 15).

After this, Obadiah finally exercised faith and did as Elijah requested. Ahab then went out to meet Elijah. I believe that Elijah's oath inspired faith in Obadiah. For the first time, Obadiah was willing to do something directly related to the Lord's testimony—he told Ahab where he could find God's prophet.

Gathering at Mount Carmel

When Ahab arrived, he immediately accused Elijah, saying, "Is this you, you troubler of Israel?" (1 Kings 18:17). He didn't blame himself but Elijah for the lack of rain. Elijah responded, "I have not troubled Israel, but you and your father's house have, because you have forsaken the commandments of the Lord and you have followed the Baals" (v. 18). When Elijah prophesied that the dew and rain would cease, it was not to bring trouble upon the people and the land but to stand for the Lord's testimony. The drought was intended to cause the people to repent and return to the Lord their God.

Having answered Ahab's accusation, Elijah then gave him a command, saying, "Send and gather to me all Israel at Mount Carmel, together with 450 prophets of Baal and 400 prophets of the Asherah, who eat at Jezebel's table" (v. 19). Ahab did so, and a huge crowd of three parties gathered together there. The smallest party was Elijah. He may not have been completely alone, for he had a servant (v. 43). Opposing them were 850 false prophets. The largest party—Ahab with the people of Israel—probably stood back a little to see what would take place between these first two groups.

A marvelous confrontation took place on Mount Carmel. The name "Carmel" means "A green field; vineyard; fruitful" (Potts, p. 62). Elijah chose a meaningful place for all the people to come together. It was a green, fruitful, and pleasant place, like a garden or vineyard. It was a mountain, elevated above the rest of the land. As such, Mount Carmel was a miniature of the entire good land.

Mount Carmel is located in the northwest corner of Israel, in the portion belonging to the tribe of Asher. In Jacob's blessing upon his sons, he said that Asher would "yield royal dainties," meaning extremely fine food fit for a king (Gen. 49:20). The same Hebrew word for Carmel is translated "fertile field" in Isaiah 32: "righteousness will abide in the fertile field" (v. 16). Elijah chose a perfect place, full of spiritual meaning. Ahab would have chosen Samaria, the capital. The false prophets may have chosen Dan or Bethel, because those were the national centers of worship. Yet Elijah chose a mountain that was a garden and a fruitful field, a place of righteousness located in the land that yielded dainties for the king. This was a good place to build an altar to the Lord and offer something that would satisfy the Lord, their God and King.

A Choice

In this wonderful place, Elijah rebuked the children of Israel and offered them a challenge, saying, "How long will you hesitate between two opinions? If the Lord is God, follow Him; but if Baal, follow him" (1 Kings 18:21). This is a crucial principle. If we are going to love the world, then we should love the world absolutely, but if we are going to love God, then we should give ourselves fully to Him. The Lord would rather that we were hot or cold, not lukewarm (Rev. 3:15–16). We shouldn't play games with our life.

The people did not answer him a word. Elijah was demanding that they make a choice, but the people of Israel must have regarded him with stony expressions. It had been a difficult three years for them, and surely Ahab had been telling them that Elijah was to blame. They must have been thinking, "Who are you to demand a decision from us? It's because of you that we have had no rain for three years. We don't care whether the Lord or Baal is the true God. All we want is rain so we can eat." So they looked at him without saying a word. They may have wanted to stone Elijah to death.

People are interesting. Even among God's people, few truly care for God's testimony. If we stand for God's testimony, we will be surprised to find that some among God's own people will become bothered by us. Few want to hear that the Lord is God, that is, He demands and deserves our everything. Yet the Lord is God, and either we are for Him or we are for ourselves. There is no middle ground. This was what Elijah spoke to the Israelites. He wasn't trying to please them. His only concern was that God would gain a people who would follow Him absolutely.

Elijah said to the people, "I alone am left a prophet of the Lord, but Baal's prophets are 450 men" (1 Kings 18:22). Why was Elijah the only prophet of the Lord remaining? Where were the hundred prophets of the Lord cared for by Obadiah? They must have remained in their cave. This is nearly unbelievable. They cared so much for their own lives that their lives lost meaning. Hopefully, none of us become like these prophets. God had protected and supported them for years. He must have invested much in each one of them to make them His prophets, yet it had gone to waste. When God had a need, not one of them knew how to stand up and fight for His testimony.

A Challenge

Although Elijah was the only prophet of the Lord standing there, he was bold. He asked that two oxen be brought as offerings. He could have asked for two turtledoves, because the poor were allowed to offer turtledoves. He could also have asked for lambs or goats, but oxen were the biggest, most costly sacrifice. Thus, an ox would make the biggest impression.

Elijah told the people, "Let [the prophets of Baal] choose one ox for themselves and cut it up, and place it on the wood, but put no fire under it; and I will prepare the other ox and lay it on the wood, and I will not put a fire under it. Then you call on the name of your god, and I will call on the name of the Lord, and the God who answers by fire, He is God" (1 Kings 18:23–24). Elijah permitted the prophets of Baal to choose the ox they wanted. He gave them no opportunity to make any excuses. If one ox seemed more suitable as an offering or more flammable in any way, he was willing to let them choose it. He was not relying on the ox or on any outward advantage, but on God. So he allowed them to choose first and offer first.

Imagine all those false prophets—how busy and excited they must have been! The four hundred prophets of the Asherah might have joined in to help the prophets of Baal, so a large crowd of people was rushing around to build an altar and to prepare the ox for offering. Perhaps they were happy for the opportunity to prove their god was real. They were praying and shouting, and they began to dance and to leap around. It must have been like watching a thousand foolish monkeys!

When we leap at the opportunity to give our life to something other than God and sing its praises, we are doing the same. Some have great faith in the financial world, placing their trust in Wall Street and the Dow Jones. Those who follow false gods place their hope in them, just as investors did in the stock market before the great crash of 1929.

The prophets of Baal all began to call on their god, but nothing happened. Perhaps they thought they weren't praying earnestly enough, so they all got down on their knees together. Still nothing happened. Maybe they began to check with each other about whether they had sinned or offended Baal. I believe they were truly disappointed that no fire came from heaven to consume their sacrifice. Eventually they became so desperate that they began to cut themselves until blood gushed out all over them (v. 28).

What a moment, when all the vanity and falseness of idolatry is exposed! It is easy to lead people into idolatry, because it is filled with people who appear to be happy with it. Yet regardless of how many people have pursued and supported such falsehood, in the end only the Lord will be found to be true and worthy of our life and worship.

Elijah highlighted this for all the people by mocking the prophets as they prayed, lept about, and cut themselves. The more frustrated they became, the more he mocked them (v. 27). His mocking words helped all the people to see how false and empty their idolatry had been. He desired to tear down the false testimony of Baal until nothing of it remained in the hearts of the people.

4

Victory and
Judgment at Carmel

A Vain Pursuit

After Elijah had gathered all the people upon Mount Carmel to the contest to prove whether the Lord or Baal was the one true God, he let the prophets of Baal offer first to see if the god they worshiped could prove himself by accepting their sacrifice by fire. He let them waste most of the day to put on a great show for the people. They were shouting loudly and leaping about to gain the attention of their god. Baal had many followers among the Israelites who surely were hoping for some sign of fire upon his offering. As time passed, however, nothing happened. Therefore, Elijah began to mock them, saying, "Call out with a loud voice, for he is a god; either he is occupied or gone aside, or is on a journey, or perhaps he is asleep and needs to be awakened" (1 Kings 18:27). The more Elijah mocked, the more desperate Baal's prophets became, even cutting themselves with knives so that blood gushed out all over them. The people must have been spellbound by such a spectacle. But in spite of this, all their shouting, leaping, praying, and bleeding came to nothing.

Just as the prophets of Baal went all out for their false god, we may give our entire lives for a career, committing ourselves to the vanity it represents, rather than serving the living and true God. Who and what rules over our lives, and what is the result? Although the worship of falsehood by so many makes it seem like it must be real, the time will come when it will be shown for what it is—vanity.

After the prophets of Baal exhausted themselves, Elijah told the people to gather to him (v. 30). Perhaps he had to do this because the people didn't like him. In their minds, he was responsible for the drought that was ravaging their land. Many of them must have been thinking, "Because of you we have suffered, our children have suffered, and we are in grave danger of starving to death!" While the prophets of Baal were praying and leaping, many of the people probably hoped that Elijah would be defeated. Rather than caring for God and His testimony, they hoped only for the outcome that they thought would make them happy and their lives easier. When they finally realized that Baal was powerless, they were willing to draw near to Elijah and the God he stood for.

Restoring the Altar of the Lord

When it was Elijah's turn, he didn't pray, jump, or do anything drastic. Instead, he simply began to repair the altar of the Lord, which had fallen into disrepair (1 Kings 18:30). The first time I read through the Bible, I was struck by how easily God's testimony among His people can be lost. The condition of the altar here represented the condition of God's testimony. The Lord had an altar where His people could present their offerings to Him. Over time, other things crept in that turned the hearts of the people away from God, even to the point that these things replaced God.

Our church life should bear the testimony of the altar of the Lord. It should be a place where we can offer ourselves to God, but when we begin to offer ourselves to other things, the Lord's testimony is compromised.

Many consecrate themselves to God, offering strong prayers that He would receive them for His use. Later, this consecration is forgotten, and they offer themselves to something else instead. Today we may intend to pursue God and to give ourselves for His purpose, but tomorrow a career, music, movies, or one of many other items in the world may steal us away. The altar we build to the Lord can quickly become damaged.

Our consecration is unreliable and always in danger of being compromised. We need to continually restore and rebuild it, because it will not remain in good repair for long. No matter how inspiring a conference is, we eventually go home. No matter how spiritual a book is, we will have to put it down. When we return to our schools, jobs, or families, we may find ourselves building altars to things other than God. Without realizing it, the altar we built to the Lord has been damaged. We may build an altar to an advanced degree, to a promotion, or to financial success. These things become our Baal. No matter how good or promising these things seem, in the end, whatever Baal we give our worship to will never be able to send down fire onto the altar we have built to his name.

Only one solitary man represented God on Mount Carmel. Elijah had spent years in isolation. None of the people understood him. Even Obadiah did not fully appreciate him. God's people had been busy building altars to the false gods in their lives and had allowed the altar of the Lord to be torn down. But now that the falseness of Baal worship had been exposed, this lonely prophet began to repair the altar in the sight of all the people.

All true spiritual things begin with the repairing of the altar of the Lord. In his message titled, "The Life of the Altar and the Tent," Watchman Nee says, "Have any of you failed? Have any of you gone down into Egypt, so that now you have your own interests and your own aspirations? If you are seeking the way of recovery, you will find it at the altar and the tent" (Nee, pp. 151–152). Our Christian life begins at the altar. The world has captured enough people to run after degrees, positions, and financial success. The Lord did not save us to be consumed on such altars. Our life is to be offered to the Lord on His altar. Since we have already consecrated ourselves to the Lord, when our consecration falls into disrepair, we do not need to build the altar. We only need to restore it. We gave ourselves to the Lord in the past, but if our consecration is in disrepair today, we must raise it back up. Then we can begin again to walk before the Lord and bear His testimony.

The Twelve Stones of the Altar

When Elijah began to repair God's altar, he "took twelve stones according to the number of the tribes of the sons of Jacob" (1 Kings 18:31). These twelve stones signified all of God's people. The altar did not belong to Elijah but was the altar of God's testimony. Therefore, it had to include every tribe. Today, we must be able to include every one of the Lord's believers in our church life if it is to be the Lord's testimony.

Elijah had God's kingdom in view, so despite the degradation that had occurred among God's people, he still used twelve stones. Perhaps we would have had a hard time using twelve stones, for we might have at least been tempted to reject Reuben. Anyone who reads Genesis can see that Reuben was terrible (Gen. 35:22; 49:3–4). He might not seem good enough to us to be a stone in God's altar. Also, how could Dan have been used for the altar of God? Dan was compared to a serpent (Gen. 49:17) because Satan would work directly through that tribe to bring in idolatry (Judg. 18:30–31; 1 Kings 12:26–30). But we are not allowed to be selective or exclusive. We may have preferred to use only the strong, healthy tribes, such as Judah and Benjamin. Perhaps we would have liked to promote Aaron's family as a substitute for some tribe. God's purpose and testimony are so inclusive, however, that even the tribes we don't like, such as Dan, bear the same preciousness as the better tribes, such as Judah.

The twelve stones of the altar of the Lord represented all of God's people. This altar today represents all believers, for God's testimony encompasses every regenerated person. If we want to be for God's testimony, we must see how inclusive the body of Christ is. We must struggle against having a small or exclusive view of His body. Our consecration is on behalf of the entire body. All God's redeemed people are included in His testimony, even those who do not yet clearly see it. In Christ, there is neither Jew nor Gentile (Gal. 3:28). In Christ, there are no Pentecostal Christians, nor Baptist Christians, nor any other kind. There are only Christians. Everyone who has received the divine life is included in this marvelous altar. Our consecration is not on behalf of some segment of God's people but on behalf of the whole body. It is for every one of God's people.

A Trench around the Altar

After using the twelve stones to rebuild the altar, Elijah dug a trench all the way around it (1 Kings 18:32). Mount Carmel had been defiled by worship to other gods, and this trench separated the altar of the Lord from the altar of Baal, from all the idols that filled the land, and from all the filthiness and corruption that polluted it. The trench indicated that the altar of the Lord belonged only to God Himself.

Such a separation is also needed in our church life. Suppose a Christian brother is gifted with administrative ability. He has consecrated himself to the Lord, so he is on the altar. He has given his time and gift to serve the church. Then one day Satan comes in. He does not look like Satan but comes in the guise of the vice president of his department at work. This is how the world works. The VP tells him, "You are the most talented organizer we have. Can you please organize our department party this year?" So the brother climbs down off the altar of the Lord and offers his time and gift to his department. During the next several weeks while he is busy running around, he has no time to serve the church. This is what happens when the altar has no trench. If there is a trench, when Satan comes to tempt us to give our life and time to something other than God, we have no way to slide off the altar, for there is a moat surrounding it.

Young people are especially vulnerable to such temptations. They consecrate themselves repeatedly. They rebuild the altar to the Lord in their lives many times. For example, they may consecrate themselves at a Christian conference, but as soon as they go back to school, they return to serving the world. This is because they have never dug a trench around the altar they built to the Lord.

After we have given ourselves to the Lord and gone back to the world time and again, we will see what the world is. The Lord will show us how filthy, corrupt, and full of idols it is. Even in the good land, many idols were brought in. Therefore, we must dig a trench to separate ourselves from all the unhealthiness. Then, as we offer ourselves more and more to God on the altar, there will be a dividing line to keep out all the subtle things of the world that threaten our consecration. Once there is a trench surrounding the altar, we will be able to befriend all kinds of people, yet we will be kept separated from whatever defiling things they are involved in.

Two Measures of Seed

The trench that Elijah dug around the altar was "large enough to hold two measures of seed" (1 Kings 18:32). How precious the Bible is! It does not say, for instance, that the trench could contain one hundred gallons of water. Instead, it says it could contain two measures of seed. This is a marvelous and meaningful description. What followed from the separating trench was not death but the seed of life coming forth out of that trench.

Our separation from the world gives us the ground to plant many seeds in those around us. I knew a Christian brother who was a senior at Taiwan University when I was there. Thirty years later, his department held a reunion which he attended. Everyone was given the opportunity to give a short speech. All of his classmates took the opportunity to boast in their careers and to enumerate their successes. One had even become the president of the University of California at Berkeley. When it came time for the brother to speak, however, he didn't seek to impress his audience with a list of his worldly accomplishments. Instead he said, "I have nothing to say, except that I believe in Jesus Christ. We all need a Savior. You too need Jesus." Without a trench to separate him from the vain things his classmates were wallowing in, he would have had no way to plant such a seed as this. His separation enabled him to become a blessing to others.

The trench around the altar had a capacity of two measures of seed. The number two in the Bible represents testimony. In order to bear the Lord's testimony, one alone is not enough. It takes two—God together with one who is consecrated to Him. Together they bear the responsibility to uplift God's testimony. When we build an altar to give ourselves to God and dig a trench to separate ourselves unto Him, God is able to produce many seeds that will bring forth life in those around us.

In these few verses, we have seen four great principles concerning God's testimony. First, it is related to His altar. If we are not willing to give ourselves to the Lord completely, we can have nothing to do with His testimony. Second, this one altar is built with twelve stones, indicating that God's testimony is on behalf of all His people. Third, this testimony requires a trench dug around it, separating it from all that is in the world. Finally, this separation produces seed that the one who works together with God may sow among the people in the world. This produces life in them. If we desire to bring others into the experience of God's testimony, we must be given to it, stand in it, be separated unto it, and sow the seed of life into others.

A Consuming Fire

After rebuilding the altar, Elijah arranged the wood upon the altar of the Lord, cut up the ox, and put its pieces upon the wood (1 Kings 18:33). Seemingly, all was ready for him to ask the Lord to send fire upon the offering. Instead, he ordered, "Fill four pitchers with water and pour it on the burnt offering and on the wood" (v. 34). He had this done three times, then filled the trench with water. Even then, he did not pray or ask the Lord to send the fire. He waited until the time appointed for the evening offering.

It is hard to believe that Elijah could be this patient, but he did everything according to God's appointed time. God had ordained a set time for certain offerings in the Old Testament. Elijah waited for the hour set for the evening offering in order to fulfill the principle of acting at the time appointed by God. In the New Testament age, God's appointed time is when His Spirit is working and speaking.

At God's appointed time, Elijah began to pray, "O Lord, the God of Abraham, Isaac and Israel, today let it be known that You are God in Israel and that I am Your servant and I have done all these things at Your word. Answer me, O Lord, answer me, that this people may know that You, O Lord, are God, and that You have turned their heart back again" (1 Kings 18:36–37).

Elijah did not address God as the God of Abraham, Isaac, and Jacob, but rather as the God of Abraham, Isaac, and Israel. God changed Jacob's name from Jacob, meaning "heel-holder" or "supplanter" (Gen. 25:26; 27:36) to Israel, meaning "a prince with God, prevailing with God" (Farrar, p. 122). He did this for the sake of His testimony. Since Elijah's prayer was absolutely for God's testimony, he used the name "Israel." The content of His prayer was that God would recapture His people and turn their hearts back to Him. He didn't pray, "O Lord, teach these stubborn people a lesson!" Instead, he prayed that God would turn their hearts from Baal back to the Lord.

After Elijah prayed, "the fire of the Lord fell and consumed the burnt offering and the wood and the stones and the dust, and licked up the water that was in the trench" (1 Kings 18:38). When the fire fell, it did not kill the people or burn up the mountainside. However, it was an intense fire. When it fell on the offering, it consumed the offering, the altar, and even the dust.

Everything we put on the altar will be consumed by such a fire. When we pray to give ourselves to the Lord, we place ourselves and our whole life on that altar. One day the Lord will send such a consuming fire to burn our offering. Look at Elijah's offering—nothing was left at all, except perhaps a pleasing fragrance to God.

Once the consuming fire fell, "all the people...fell on their faces; and they said, 'The Lord, He is God; the Lord, He is God'" (v. 39). The reaction produced through Elijah's work was much more than Obadiah had ever produced. The Lord had worked so hard to gain a man to be for His testimony. If He can gain even one such as Elijah to stand for His testimony, the hearts of all the people can be turned back to Him.

As the people were repenting, Elijah acted quickly. He commanded that the false prophets be seized. There must have been a great struggle as all the Israelites ran to grab the prophets of Baal. All these prophets were then brought down to the brook Kishon and slaughtered (v. 40).

The brook Kishon is a place for overcoming. It was the place Barak fought and overcame the army of Sisera (Judg. 4:12–16). This time, however, the people of Israel came to Kishon to overcome the idolatry of the false prophets.

The Lord Sending Rain

After Elijah slaughtered all the prophets of Baal, he told Ahab, "Go up, eat and drink; for there is the sound of the roar of a heavy shower" (1 Kings 18:41). For three years there has been no rain or dew, but now Elijah was giving the word, and the Lord would send the rain.

Then Elijah went up to the top of Carmel and bowed down to the earth, putting his face between his knees. Seven times he sent his servant to look toward the sea for clouds. After the seventh time, his servant reported a little cloud the size of a man's hand.

This signifies that no matter how God is operating, whether He stops the rain or sends it, He always works together with man. No matter how great the miracle or work of power God wants to perform, He never bypasses the principle of working together with and through the hand of man. No matter how intensely God desires to build up His testimony, He still must first gain someone to cooperate with Him. This is why, when the cloud appeared, it was said to be the size of a man's hand.

As soon as Elijah heard about this little cloud, he sent his servant to King Ahab with the message, "Prepare your chariot and go down, so that the heavy shower does not stop you" (v. 44). He knew that God was not just going to send some light sprinkling of rain but rather heavy showers to water the dry land. While there was still only a tiny cloud in the sky, Elijah warned Ahab, letting him know that this was the Lord's doing through his own hand. "In a little while the sky grew black with clouds and wind, and there was a heavy shower. And Ahab rode and went to Jezreel" (v. 45). This confirmed Elijah's word to Ahab.

After Elijah sent word to Ahab, "the hand of the Lord was on Elijah, and he girded up his loins and outran Ahab to Jezreel" (v. 46). Now that the prophets of Baal were slaughtered and the rain had come, God carried Elijah along in the power of His Spirit to meet Ahab at the gate of Jezreel. This was the final punctuation mark to all that God had accomplished through Elijah in this stage of his service. That Elijah arrived at Jezreel before Ahab was a confirming miracle that Elijah had truly been God's prophet. No matter how great a man Elijah was, he could never have outrun the king's best horses. Ahab was forced to realize that none of the things that had happened those three years, nor the great events of that day, could have been carried out by anyone other than the God of Elijah.

I think this verse is for young believers, because they get excited about beginning things for the Lord, but often fail to finish what they have begun. For example, they may easily become stirred up to preach the gospel or to begin a Bible study on their campus, but after a few days or weeks, they quietly let those matters drop. Elijah didn't let anything drop but instead brought this entire matter of withholding the rain and the dew to its close.

Jezebel's Threat and Elijah's Flight

After all that the Lord did through him, Elijah must again have been feeling very victorious. He probably was filled with praise to the Lord, but very likely also overly appreciated his own role. Perhaps Elijah commented to his servant, "I never expected that I would become so used by the Lord. What a work the Lord did through me at Mount Carmel!"

As soon as Ahab arrived home, his wife Jezebel apparently asked him, "What happened? For three years there has been no rain, and now all of a sudden there is this downpour." Then "Ahab told Jezebel all that Elijah had done, and how he had killed all the prophets with the sword" (1 Kings 19:1).

Ahab might have been impressed by Elijah and begun to consider him a man of God. He may have even begun to realize that the Lord was the true God. But Jezebel had no such turn of heart. As soon as Ahab told her that all of her prophets had been slaughtered, she became furious. She might have told Ahab, "How could you let this happen? If all the prophets of Baal are slain, what does that say of me?" Therefore, she sent this message to Elijah: "So may the gods do to me and even more, if I do not make your life as the life of one of them by tomorrow about this time" (v. 2).

Jezebel's messenger must have been afraid to deliver such a message to Elijah. All the people were probably talking about how Elijah had called down fire and how so many false prophets had been slain. The messenger must have been trembling as he knocked on Elijah's door. Inside, Elijah may have been reliving every detail of his glorious victory. Just as he was enjoying his mocking of the false prophets and rebuilding of God's altar, he heard someone knocking. Perhaps he thought the elders of Israel had come to congratulate him or recognize him with an award. Instead, there stood one of Jezebel's slaves with a death threat.

What a shock! When Elijah heard Jezebel's threat, he lost all his boldness and buoyancy and immediately fled, along with his servant (v. 3). They probably didn't even take time to prepare for the journey but just fled for their lives. His experience went from bold triumph to cowardly retreat! Yet the Lord would use such an experience to bring him into another stage of growth.

5

The Perfecting
of Elijah (1)

Elijah's Need after Mount Carmel

Elijah was an interesting prophet; either what he did was dramatic, or he did nothing at all. His story begins with his bold declaration to the king of Israel that there would be no rain or dew except by his word. Then for more than three years, he lived quietly, first by the brook Cherith and then in Zarepharh. During all that time, Elijah did little but patiently grow under the Lord's dealing. Then one day he suddenly came to Mount Carmel, where he defeated all the prophets of Baal. On that one day eight hundred fifty false prophets were slain, and the Lord was vindicated in the eyes of all Israel. After this marvelous victory, however, God took Elijah away again to work with him further.

Elijah's challenge to the prophets of Baal is one of the most interesting and dramatic stories in the Bible. Every such event requires a further and deeper dealing before the Lord. Everyone can appreciate Elijah's victory over the false prophets. It may inspire us even to the point that we wish we could do such a great deed. Some may wish that they had been born in those days so they could have seen the spectacle. For Elijah, this time of miracle-working was a time of revelation and heavenly vision. We like exciting events, but exciting events don't really grant us the substantiation we need for spiritual growth.

In fact, Elijah's marvelous victory was somewhat hollow. Although the people finally admitted that the Lord was the true God and that Baal was false, not much changed in their hearts. They acknowledged the Lord but did not follow Him. Therefore, Elijah's victory did not actually cause the people to turn their hearts to the Lord. Even fire coming down from heaven did not have much long-term effect. Ultimately, the real matter in this story was not the impact on the people, but the impact upon Elijah himself.

Any time we have a spiritual victory, we must pass through a deeper experience to substantiate it. This is true of any spiritual attainment or revelation. The heavenly vision we see and the enjoyment of Christ that we possess require that we experience something further for their substantiation.

The same is true in every aspect of life. Recent graduates from an engineering program may be full of knowledge, but they need experience to back up their education. Even those who were the best in their class need to go through the process of making mistakes and then being criticized by their bosses and colleagues. Only after working in their chosen field for many years can they really look back and appreciate the value of their education. Thus, God took Elijah through a time of further training after his victorious experience at Mount Carmel.

Elijah's Cowardly Flight

God began by exposing Elijah's real condition. Elijah seemed to be very bold. After all, had he not just stood up to eight hundred fifty false prophets in the presence of all the people? However, compare Elijah to the prophets of Baal. They were willing to die for their false idols, whereas Elijah, who had the real and living God, quickly ran away when threatened by Jezebel. He ran all the way to Beersheba, on the far side of the kingdom of Judah, close to the wilderness on the south (1 Kings 19:3). Once he was outside of Jezebel's sphere of influence, he should have felt safe. Elijah could have asked King Jehoshaphat of Judah for asylum, but in his anxiety for his life, apparently he did not trust even him.

Thus it seems that Elijah still loved and treasured himself. When he was upon Mount Carmel declaring the name of the Lord, he appeared powerful and victorious, but immediately afterward he showed himself to be a coward. Beersheba was a place where God declared His faithfulness (Gen. 26:23–24). When Elijah arrived there, he should have been able to trust in God's faithfulness, knowing He would keep him. Instead, he seems to have asked his servant, "Can you still run?" Perhaps his servant answered, "Elijah, my legs are too tired and swollen to run any more." Elijah may have said, "I am still strong, so I will keep on running without you until I find a place where nobody can find me."

Elijah ran to the wilderness outside the good land. Even far away in the wilderness, however, Elijah was still anxious for his life. He may have thought, "Jezebel was very angry. Surely she will send men to find me. They could be here any moment. But where else can I flee, seeing I am already in the wilderness? If I must die, I would rather the Lord take my life than be killed by Jezebel." So he sat down under a juniper tree and asked God to let him die, saying, "It is enough; now, O Lord, take my life, for I am not better than my fathers" (1 Kings 19:4).

In principle, whenever we begin to care for God's testimony as Elijah did on Mount Carmel, difficulties will come. A life lived for God's testimony is filled with more threats and troubles than any other kind of life is. This is why Elijah asked the Lord to take his life. It was at this point that the angel of God came to him and told him to eat, showing him some bread baked on hot stones and a jug of water. A little later, the angel of the Lord came to him again and said, "Arise, eat, because the journey is too great for you" (1 Kings 19:7). After Elijah ate, he was able to run for forty more days and forty nights. In the Bible, forty is a number that signifies being tried, tested, or tempted. Elijah ran those forty days and nights all the way to Mount Horeb, the mountain of God, where he found a cave and hid himself. Finally, Elijah felt safe enough to stop running. How cowardly he seems! He should have written an autobiography called The Chicken Prophet to show us how such a great, victorious prophet could become so defeated.

Growing through Defeat

All this happened to help Elijah know who he was. After we give a good testimony and people seem to be helped, aren't we proud of ourselves? We may think we are better than others. After Elijah finished his work at Mount Carmel, he must have had a very high estimation of himself. He needed to see that everything he did was due to the Lord's grace. It was His mercy and grace that carried him through. The Lord would not allow him to steal the glory for himself.

This is not only true for Elijah. When we serve the church, others may tell us how much they appreciate what we have done. The first time we hear this, it may not leave much impression, but the second time, we begin to pay attention. After three others tell us this, we begin to think it must be true. We might even tell God, "Did You see the great job I did for You? You would be so limited without me, but since I am here, You can accomplish so much." Whenever our heart is lifted up like this, God must show us who we really are. The entire time Elijah was running away from Jezebel, God was showing him who he really was.

We don't mature spiritually through high, spiritual victories like that on Mount Carmel but through defeats, even after running away like Elijah did. It is when we pass through experiences of defeat that we begin to seek Him. Once we discover that we can only rely on Him, we will truly treasure Him.

Many think that growth in the Lord is obtained cheaply. They think that since Christ is always available, they can turn to Him at their convenience. When they are in the mood to enjoy the Lord, He will be there. If they have a problem, He is able to fix it for them. They have a "Santa Claus" Jesus. If we have such an attitude, the Lord Jesus may purposely hide Himself from us. When we finally become aware that we have lost the Lord's presence, we will realize that what He seeks in us is not cheap. If we want to follow and gain Him, we must pay a price. If we want to stand firm with Him, we must pay a price—we do not have a cheap Christ. Paying the necessary price often involves being exposed, frustrated, bothered, and even becoming unclear for a period of time. If we pay the price to follow the Lord, however, every defeat and difficulty will cause us to grow to another stage of life.

Hiding in a Cave on the Mountain of God

Elijah ran forty days and nights to Mount Horeb, where he found a cave and lodged there (1 Kings 19:9). Don't think that when he finally arrived at God's mountain he had learned anything. Instead of finding God there, he only found a cave. A cave is a shelter created and provided by God. To dwell in a cave costs nothing. Elijah's dwelling in a cave is a picture of our not paying any price to follow the Lord and grow. Obadiah managed to hide a hundred prophets of the Lord in a cave, yet they never paid the price for God's testimony. What God needs is not cave dwellers but those who will stand for Him.

Elijah stopped running at Mount Horeb, the mountain of God. He had come from Mount Carmel, a green and fruitful place filled with the Lord's blessing, to the mountain of God, the place where he should have realized that his only need was God Himself. Instead of coming to God alone and taking Him as his shelter, protection, guard, and defense, he hid in a cave, trusting in it to protect him from his enemies.

Using the Church Life as Our Cave

Often we can find a comfortable cave in our church life where we find a peaceful and safe refuge from our problems. It is good to experience peace with our fellow members in the family of God, yet what happens when we no longer feel the need for such a refuge? When we are frightened or anxious because of problems in our life, we flee to our church-life cave. But as soon as our life becomes less turbulent, we no longer feel there is any need for it, and we are gone. For example, when some have no job, they attend all the church meetings and pray about their situation. As soon as they find a job, however, they disappear. When we are in trouble we pray much, but when the trouble subsides, we may feel free to do whatever we want, with no consideration for the Lord's need. If so, we are in a cave, caring only for our own peacefulness.

Elijah's Complaint and God's Reply

This is why God had to appear to Elijah and ask him, "What are you doing here, Elijah?" (1 Kings 19:9). Elijah was God's anointed prophet. He represented God's testimony and upheld His desire on the earth. Yet here he was, defeated and hiding in a cave. Elijah answered, "I have been very zealous for the Lord, the God of hosts; for the sons of Israel have forsaken Your covenant, torn down Your altars and killed Your prophets with the sword. And I alone am left; and they seek my life, to take it away" (v. 10). He seemed to be implying that if the Lord were a good God, these things would never have happened. If He was trustworthy, Elijah wouldn't be the only one left.

If I were in this situation, I would have answered, "Lord, let me tell You honestly, I am afraid of Jezebel. She has people killed without even batting an eye. That terrible woman gave orders to have me murdered, and that's why I'm hiding in this cave." But even in his defeated condition, Elijah's response to God was to justify himself rather than admit the real situation.

Perhaps we have told the Lord, "You are always so wise, but in this particular case, You were a little foolish. Had You done it my way, things would have turned out better. Now the situation is so messy that I'm not sure even You can rescue it." This feeling may be hidden in our heart while we pray our godly prayers. It is better to be honest and tell God what we think. Perhaps we feel like telling God that all the messes in our life are His fault. When we are honest like this, at least God can expose us. In the end, the more we are genuine and honest with God, the more He will be able to bless us.

God answered Elijah with a strong wind, an earthquake, and a fire—all things related to God's government (vv. 11–12). After God told Elijah to stand on the mountain, there was a great, strong wind that split the mountains and broke the rocks. Following this there was an earthquake, followed again by a fire. God was telling Elijah that He was in control. If He could cause this great wind, earthquake, and fire, He could also handle Elijah's situation. The degraded situation in Israel was not a mistake. God was still Lord over all.

The Lord, however, was not in the wind, nor in the earthquake, nor in the fire. It was not His intention to come to Elijah in an outward show of power. Instead, He preferred to come to Elijah in the New Testament principle of "a still small voice" (v. 12, KJV). Then, the Lord asked him once again, "What are you doing here, Elijah?" (v. 13).

It is hard to believe that Elijah would answer the same way he did the first time. It seems that once people make up their minds to argue with God, they won't change regardless of how God approaches them. Elijah repeated his answer to God, saying "I have been very zealous for the Lord, the God of hosts; for the sons of Israel have forsaken Your covenant, torn down Your altars and killed Your prophets with the sword. And I alone am left; and they seek my life, to take it away" (v. 14). It seems Elijah thought God had been asleep and needed to wake up.

God's Continuing Work with Elijah

The Lord did not argue with Elijah. Arguments do not work against such stubbornness. Nor did He perform any more miracles to teach him anything further. The wind, earthquake, and fire had already displayed God's power and authority. Instead, the Lord did something to reveal His great wisdom—He gave Elijah an additional commitment, telling him to anoint three people. This commitment would bring Elijah on to maturity.

This was part of the bigger picture of how God was dealing with Elijah. There are three steps to knowing God. First, we know Him through His actions and deeds. Then, we know Him through His ways and operating principles. Finally, we know God Himself. Previously, Elijah had known God according to His actions, such as withholding the dew and the rain. Then through God's dealings with him at the brook Cherith and with the widow at Zarephath, Elijah came to know God's ways by being dealt with and humbled, by learning to rely on His provision, and by witnessing the operation of resurrection life.

Now God wanted Elijah to see who He was. He had passed through trials and dealings. Having been exposed through his defeat in running from Jezebel and again through his arguing with God, he was finally ready to know God Himself. God had revealed Himself as Elijah's divine provider. Even when he shamefully ran to the wilderness in his worst defeat, God fed him and gave him rest under the juniper tree. To let Elijah know that He was in control of everything in the universe, God demonstrated His authority through the wind, the earthquake, and the fire. Finally, He came to Elijah as a gentle, quiet voice so he could know Him directly.

Yet even after all this, Elijah continued to argue with God and even made accusations against Him. Working with Elijah was harder than working with Balaam's donkey (Num. 22). When God told the donkey to speak, it simply spoke, but Elijah insisted on his own ways and views. He obeyed God by preaching to Ahab, but now he was trying to preach to God. This showed Elijah's stubbornness and immaturity. This didn't cause God to give up on Elijah. What He began with him, He would complete. Although Elijah was scared, selfish, and stubborn, God continued to work with him until he matured. To this end, God give him a further commitment so that he might mature as a man of God.

Further Commitment

The first part of God's instruction to Elijah was to return through the wilderness to Damascus to anoint Hazael as king over Aram (1 Kings 19:15). Damascus was the capital of Aram, the enemy of both Israel and Judah. Had He told Elijah, "Go back to Israel and be My prophet," Elijah may not have had the strength and courage to obey. Since Elijah was so concerned with his own safety, God sent him to a place where Jezebel could not reach him. Isn't God merciful? Elijah could find political asylum among the Arameans, and through him, God would appoint a new king over them

Hazael means "God beheld, or has seen" (Potts, p. 107). Even in a Gentile country, apart from God's chosen people, God sees. If we are bothered by the political situation, we shouldn't be anxious—God sees. If we are treated unfairly, we shouldn't worry—God sees and rules over all.

Besides anointing the Aramean king, God told Elijah to anoint Jehu as the next king of Israel (1 Kings 19:16). Though the first part of this commitment was comforting to Elijah, placing him far from Jezebel's grasp, the second part—anointing Jehu as king to replace Ahab—must have seemed like a death warrant to him. Once Ahab heard of this, he would rise up to kill Elijah. In giving this command, God indicated His intent to rule not only over the Gentiles but even more over His own people.

Jehu means "Jehovah is He" (Potts, p. 134). In the Gentile countries, God merely sees all things. But among God's people in the good land, Jehovah is God. The name Jehovah refers to the God who is carrying out His purpose. In our church life, we should never forget that God has a purpose and plan. Just as Elijah complained about the situation in Israel, we may be concerned about the deteriorating condition of the church. However, we must remember that God is still carrying out His purpose in the church.

Raising Up a Replacement

As the final part of His commitment for Elijah, God told him, "Elisha the son of Shaphat of Abel-meholah you shall anoint as prophet in your place" (1 Kings 19:16). Elisha was to be Elijah's replacement. God's commitment had three parts. Each of God's instructions was more difficult than the previous one. From Elijah's point of view, the first part was relatively safe, since it sent him far from Jezebel. The second part seemed hazardous, since it involved returning to Israel. But this third part made it seem that God was giving him up and replacing him. This is the greatest lesson anyone can learn.

Nobody wants to be replaced. Yet God asked Elijah to obediently anoint his own replacement. The normal human response to such a word would be to vow to be more obedient, faithful, and diligent in service so that there would be no need to be replaced. This time, however, Elijah didn't argue with God.

Which was more spiritual—Elijah's performing of great miracles in the Lord's name or his acceptance of this final commitment from the Lord? Elijah's exercise was powerful.

He had stopped the rain from falling from the heavens. He had dried up the dew. Through him the widow had been supplied with food and her son raised from the dead. He had called down fire from heaven. He had slaughtered all the prophets of Baal. Who was more spiritual—this powerful and victorious Elijah, or the defeated, totally exposed Elijah who was willing to anoint his own replacement? Nobody wants to be replaced, but he did it. This displays Elijah's spiritual maturity. It is hard to find someone who is willing to be laid aside and replaced, but Elijah was willing. In fact, he did more than come to Elisha and pour oil on his head. He did not tell Elisha, "Since you are God's prophet now, let Him train you. Don't ask me for any help." Instead, he trained Elisha to be his replacement. He became Elisha's teacher to help him learn how to carry God's testimony.

Because Elijah was so mature and handled God's commitment in such a spiritual manner, God was able to introduce the principle of His New Testament economy through Elisha. Elijah stood for the testimony of the Lord, but there was too much raw power, fire, and death in his prophethood. Elijah's works of power expressed God's divinity and judgment but not the humanity of Christ.

With Elisha, however, God was able to operate differently. Elisha was the son of Shaphat, which means "He judged; a judge" (Potts, p. 215). Like Elijah, Elisha also judged, but he judged from Abel-meholah, which means "place of mirth; meadow of dancing" (Potts, p. 14). This was a different kind of judging. In Elisha's judging, there was no need for him to slaughter anyone or to call down fire. He could simply point to the God of grace who was so wonderful. By enjoying Him in the meadow of dancing, people would be empowered to drop their idols and repent of their sinfulness. Here, God would be their wonderful Savior. This was the way of judging that God sought to introduce. It was only made possible through Elijah's willingness to receive such a commitment from the Lord.

6

The Perfecting
of Elijah (2)

God Trusts Himself, Not Us

God trained Elijah after his victory on Carmel firstly, by allowing him to be exposed by running from Jezebel, and secondly, by causing him to see who He Himself is. In providing Elijah with food and water in the wilderness, God showed that He was the divine provider. In showing Elijah the wind, earthquake, and fire, He revealed His divine government. In speaking to Elijah in a gentle, quiet voice, He was coming to Elijah according to the New Testament principle.

After this training, however, Elijah still lacked something. Twice God asked him, "What are you doing here, Elijah?" (1 Kings 19:9, 13). Each time, Elijah answered, "I have been very zealous for the Lord, the God of hosts; for the sons of Israel have forsaken Your covenant, torn down Your altars and killed Your prophets with the sword. And I alone am left; and they seek my life, to take it away" (vv. 10, 14). This is the answer of someone who was under an enormous amount of pressure. Elijah was suffering psychological distress.

In spiritual warfare, God needs someone to fight on His side. Elijah had been such a fighter for the Lord. Think of how Elijah stood before the four hundred fifty prophets of Baal on Mount Carmel. As they were leaping, shouting, and cutting themselves, he mocked them. After he rebuilt the altar of the Lord, he had water poured upon the altar and into the trench. All of this was Elijah's strong contending for the Lord. He commanded fire to come down from heaven and consume the offering. Afterward, he led the people to lay hold of the prophets of Baal and slaughtered them all by the brook Kishon. Such a struggle on the Lord's behalf surely must have been exhausting!

When we are serving the Lord, we experience His sustaining and supplying grace, but if we lack maturity in life, we will be affected by environmental and psychological pressure. Eventually, Elijah felt so threatened and worn out that he ran away to take refuge in a cave. This reveals that Elijah lacked maturity.

Thus, if God had trusted Elijah any further, God would have been in trouble. Elijah, as he was, could not carry out anything more of what the Lord desired. God could, however, trust in Himself. Elijah's problems, failures, and stubbornness could not hinder God. Elijah may have thought that he was able to follow and serve God because he was so good and capable. However, he was only able to follow and serve God because of who God is. Even though Elijah was stubborn and defeated, God was able to commit something further to him. God did not trust Elijah, but He trusted Himself. He was able to use Elijah because He is God.

God is able to entrust His work to us, not because we are trustworthy, but because He is. If God relied upon us to trust Him, He would be in trouble. We are totally unreliable in ourselves. Even those who seem so pure are full of problems. Yet God loves each of us. He knows our condition and is saving us. We shouldn't worry; God will use us. We can express Him and be His testimony. He doesn't trust us to do this but trusts Himself. It is impossible for us, but it is possible for God.

Seven Thousand Reserved for God

Elijah had told the Lord that he was the only one left to

stand for Him. The implication was that God needed him. God refuted Elijah's claim, saying, "I will leave 7,000 in Israel, all the knees that have not bowed to Baal and every mouth that has not kissed him" (1 Kings 19:18).

The number seven thousand is meaningful. In the Bible, the number seven signifies completion in time. Three signifies the triune God, while four signifies creation. When three (the triune God) and four (mankind) are added together, the result is the completion of what God is after in this age. God, however, did not leave merely seven for Himself, nor seventy, nor seven hundred, but seven thousand. In other words, God reserved for Himself completion in this age one thousand fold. God had more than enough people to worship Him, even if Elijah couldn't see them.

God Having Other Prophets

God was able to use other prophets besides Elijah: "A prophet approached Ahab king of Israel and said, 'Thus says the Lord, "Have you seen all this great multitude? Behold, I will deliver them into your hand today, and you shall know that I am the Lord"'" (1 Kings 20:13). When Elijah heard this, he might have became jealous—another prophet was speaking for the Lord to King Ahab, and that was supposed to be his job. Later, a "man of God" approached King Ahab, and also spoke the Lord's words to him (v. 28). Then again, God used a "man of the sons of the prophets" (which means a prophet's student or disciple) to speak to Ahab (vv. 35–42). These were surely three different men, and God used each of them to speak to Ahab during his war with the Arameans.

God seemed to be indicating to Elijah that He was not only able to use another prophet and a man of God, but even a son of the prophets, someone who is merely a prophet in training. Elijah may have thought he was special and important, but

God reserved a great complement of people for Himself. He was able to use a number of prophets who worked together for His testimony.

Suppose we held a gospel meeting, and five people were saved. Wouldn't we be excited that God used us? Then suppose we found out that another church got ten people saved. We may think, "Every time God blesses us, He blesses them more. Every time we experience some glory, their glory outshines ours. I wish God would use us rather than them."

How wise God was to train Elijah in this way! Elijah could no longer think that he was the only one standing for God, because God had left thousands of others for Himself. The Lord was able to use others to carry out His work.

Micaiah the Son of Imlah

To acknowledge that God can use others can be a difficult lesson to learn. At first, Elijah may have only grudgingly admitted that God was not restricted to using him. The other prophets God used up to this point were not significant enough to have their names recorded in the Bible. Instead, they were only referred to as "a prophet," a "man of God," and a "man of the sons of the prophets." Elijah may have taken comfort in the fact that he was still more notable than the others.

Yet a little later, God used another prophet whose name is recorded—Micaiah the son of Imlah (1 Kings 22:8). Micaiah was a prophet who only spoke what the Lord said to him, and he was not afraid to speak the word of the Lord to Ahab (v. 14). Micaiah means "Who is like to God?" (Potts, p. 172). God was showing Elijah that he was not unique and that the whole universe did not revolve around him, for Micaiah could also speak the Lord's words to the king of Israel.

God's Inclusiveness

Christians inevitably become involved with the sphere of religion. Religion is subjective to each individual. Because of religion, Christians tend to become narrower than they were before becoming religious. In religion, people tend to become insistent that only they are right and everybody else is wrong. When Pentecostal Christians speak in tongues or raise their hands to pray, are we able to fellowship with them even if we don't have the same practice? We may doubt that Pentecostal healings and tongue-speaking are real, but we must admit that most Pentecostals seek to be pure before the Lord. Are we able to appreciate that? We may feel we are more grounded in the truth than they are, but it is also possible that much of what we have learned is doctrine and not reality to us and has made us complicated. Are we simply able to love other believers?

We don't have to imitate others in order to love them. We should be careful with what the Lord has shown us. When I was young, I practiced tongue-speaking, but later the Lord revealed to me that it was not what He was after. I realized that tongues can be a gift from the Lord, but they are not His desire. We must hold on to what the Lord has shown us and be faithful to it. I will never give up the local church; I will never give up the body of Christ; I will never give up the ministry of life; and I will never give up the proper growth unto maturity. I will never give up these things, for they are what the Lord has committed to me. But neither will I say that the Lord can only do this much or that He cannot go beyond this commitment nor do something other than what He has shown me. No, the Lord is always able to do something further.

It was crucial for Elijah to see that God was not restricted to using him. Religious people always feel that they are the star of the show and that all the light should shine on them. Such people may even be willing to hold God back, saying, "God can use only me and no other." Elijah was very useful to God, but God was able to use other prophets as well. Elijah was one of the greatest prophets in the Old Testament, but God also used "a prophet," a "man of God," a "man of the sons of the prophets," and eventually Micaiah the son of Imlah. Praise the Lord that He is able to use so many servants! His work is great and unlimited.

We should never think that other Christians are useless to the Lord or look down on them. The Lord Jesus said, "He who is not against us is for us" (Mark 9:40). We should love them as our dear brothers and sisters. We are for the organic body of Christ. We are not for religious success. The practices of other Christians should never be allowed to become a frustration to fellowship. I will never join a denomination, but I love the Lord's believers in every denomination. We must have this attitude.

God was training Elijah in these basic matters. Elijah could no longer say he was the only prophet. God had prophets upon prophets upon prophets. We should not think that we are so great that God can show Himself only to us, that God can speak only to us, or that God can work only through us. God is inclusive in carrying out His purpose. Praise Him for this!

A Deceiving Spirit

Ahab, the king of Israel, asked Jehoshaphat, the king of Judah, to help him recapture the city of Ramoth-Gilead from the king of Aram. Before agreeing to this, Jehoshaphat asked Ahab to inquire of the Lord for guidance. So Ahab assembled four hundred prophets and asked them, "Shall I go against Ramoth-gilead to battle or shall I refrain?" (1 Kings 22:6). These four hundred prophets answered, "Go up, for the Lord will give it into the hand of the king" (v. 6). But Jehoshaphat was a wise man. He realized that something was wrong. All of these prophets were shouting slogans. He wanted to hear from somebody who didn't surrender to unified slogan-shouting, so he asked, "Is there not yet a prophet of the Lord here that we may inquire of him?" (v. 7). Ahab answered, "There is yet one man by whom we may inquire of the Lord, but I hate him, because he does not prophesy good concerning me, but evil. He is Micaiah son of Imlah" (v. 8).

Micaiah was a real prophet who saw a great vision. He said to Ahab, "I saw the Lord sitting on His throne, and all the host of heaven standing by Him on His right and on His left. The Lord said, 'Who will entice Ahab to go up and fall at Ramoth-gilead?' And one said this while another said that. Then a spirit came forward and stood before the Lord and said, 'I will entice him.' The Lord said to him, 'How?' And he said, 'I will go out and be a deceiving spirit in the mouth of all his prophets.' Then He said, 'You are to entice him and also prevail. Go and do so'" (vv. 19–22).

These verses are sobering. When God asked the host of heaven what to do with Ahab, maybe one suggested that Ahab should die in a chariot crash, and another suggested that he should die in battle. Then one suggested he become a deceiving spirit in the mouth of Ahab's prophets to mislead him to his doom. God responded, "Go and do so." The Lord allowed a deceiving spirit to be put in the mouth of Ahab's prophets, so there were four hundred liars speaking to the king of Israel. Each of these liars believed that he was speaking the truth. They were not merely flattering the king. They thought that what they were speaking was right. This should give us further cause to fear the Lord!

How can we know when a deceiving spirit is operating? We must not only look at the result of the prophecy but also at the process of the speaking. A deceiving spirit is focused on things to do rather than on the process of carrying out God's will. A deceiving spirit speaks according to emotion and not according to truth. A deceiving spirit focuses on activity rather than on growth in life. We must be careful when we start to focus on what should or should not be done in the church life. Our only center should be Jesus Christ our Lord.

Elijah's Replacement

Elijah's final maturing experience involved the training and equipping of Elisha. When Elijah was hiding at Mount Horeb, God told him to go to the wilderness of Damascus to anoint Hazael king of Aram. On the way, Elijah passed by the hometown of Elisha (1 Kings 19:19). This was God's arrangement. As Elijah passed by Elisha's hometown, he must have begun to consider what the Lord had committed to him. He may have had the realization that raising up his replacement was more crucial than anointing kings. He was wise, and he took the right route.

Elijah never did anoint Hazael or Jehu. It may seem strange to us that once Elijah became mature, he didn't carry out all of God's commands. God gave him three commands: (1) anoint Hazael to be king of Aram, (2) anoint Jehu to be king of Israel, and (3) anoint Elisha as his own replacement. If these commands had been given to me, I would have felt that the third command was too difficult. I might have become occupied with anointing Hazael and Jehu, perhaps spending a long time to tutor them and help them to be good kings. But Elijah didn't do this. He saw instead that the most important part in this commitment was not anointing or raising up kings, but raising up Elisha to be his replacement. He had become truly spiritual.

Some Bible scholars have said that since God commanded that he be replaced with Elisha, that Elijah must have been a failure. However, the fact that he was publicly raptured in the presence of Elisha and at least fifty others is a strong indication that he was not a failure. God honored him this way because he had become so pure toward God. Elijah had his weaknesses and problems, yet he knew how to do things in the proper order when God commanded.

Eventually, it was Elisha, Elijah's replacement, who carried out God's charge to anoint Hazael and Jehu as kings. It was not that Elijah refused to finish what God had commanded him, but he had learned that not everything spoken to him by God would be accomplished through him. God's commitment could be carried out by someone else. The important thing for him to do was to raise up Elisha as his replacement and let him anoint the two kings.

Sometimes the things God commits to us are not accomplished through us but through others. Whatever God speaks to us will be accomplished. God has committed to me the raising up of local churches. I can envision many local churches filled with young believers who love and serve the Lord fervently. They are growing in life and truth, and they bear the Lord's testimony. This dream may not be realized for another thirty or forty years, so I probably will not see it, but that doesn't matter. If we are faithful in life, truth, and loving others, forty years from now many local churches will be blossoming on the earth to welcome the Lord when He returns.

Whenever we insist, "I am it. God must use me," then all kinds of problems can arise. We may become exclusive, narrow, and very selective about who is in and who is out, and begin to judge other believers according to our standard. Remember the lesson God taught Elijah, that He is a great God with a great work. He is able to use many different people to carry out His desire.

Elisha's Response

When Elijah came to Elisha, he did not anoint him with oil. The Bible never says so. Instead, when he found the man who was to become his replacement, he threw his mantle on him (1 Kings 19:19). By covering Elisha with his mantle, he was declaring that Elisha was identified with him. When people saw Elisha, it was as though they were seeing Elijah. This mantle became the source of Elisha's authority. After Elijah threw his mantle on him, Elisha did the right thing—he followed him. Elijah didn't say anything to Elisha but simply went up to him as he was plowing the field and threw his mantle over him. This act, however, caused a dramatic reaction in Elisha (vv. 20–21). Realizing Elijah's mantle meant becoming separated to the Lord's work, he asked Elijah for permission to kiss his father and mother goodbye. Then he slaughtered the yoke of oxen he was plowing with and, burning the plowing implements to cook them, he fed everyone with the meat. Finally, he left everything to follow Elijah without any hesitation or looking back.

Ministering to Elijah

As Elisha followed Elijah, he ministered to him (1 Kings 19:21). His behavior spoke volumes. When Elijah put his mantle on him, he left everything. Then Elisha apparently gave the mantle back, for Elijah was later wearing it (2 Kings 2:8). He was content to follow and learn as long as Elijah lived, all the while ministering to him. As Elijah was teaching him the secret of having God's presence as a still small voice and the way to be faithful to God and serve Him, Elisha ministered to Elijah by serving and caring for him.

Many young Christians today have no idea what it means to minister in this way. They are ignorant of the spiritual lessons of following the Lord, for they have never learned to serve those who are caring for them and raising them up. Have we ever ministered to even one older person who has labored to help us? Often we see the older ones as lawgivers who only come to check if we have prayed and read the Bible today, or if we have preached the gospel recently. As a result, we run and hide when we see them coming. It is even worse, however, when we only seek to be served by them. This is not a healthy culture.

Elisha was not like this. He understood the principle of serving and following an older one. Rather than wearing Elijah's mantle and immediately taking his place, he gave the mantle back. Eventually, Elisha would get it back when Elijah was raptured, but in the meantime, he was content to learned from Elijah. As he attended to Elijah, he may have asked him many questions. saying, "Dear Elijah, what is your understanding of Genesis? What is the meaning of Abel's sacrifice? Why wasn't God happy with Cain's sacrifice? Why was God able to use Moses to such an extent? Oh, master, be careful on this part of the road. You can lean on me so you don't slip and fall. Now please tell me, what was your experience with God on Mount Horeb?" I assure you, that was a precious time of learning for Elisha.

We should all learn this lesson. If we never minister to those older and more mature than us, it will be harder for us to learn, grow in the Lord, and be raised up to be useful to Him. If we love to serve in this way, we will be truly blessed.

7

God's People
and God's Name

God's testimony is related to His people and His name. Two events at the end of Elijah's life show his concern for these two aspects of God's testimony. The first involved the vineyard of Naboth (1 Kings 21) and is related to God's people. The second is God's judgment on King Ahaziah (2 Kings 1), which is related to God's name. These two events were the high points of Elijah's stand as he upheld and bore God's testimony on the earth.

Concerning His testimony, God is jealous over His people and His name. This should be reflected in our church life today. Since the churches bear the Lord's testimony on the earth, our church life must focus on the believers and the name of Jesus Christ. For example, every church has its leaders, but those leaders must never replace Christ, for He alone is the Head of the church, and nothing must be allowed to replace or insult His headship. To care properly for God's testimony, we must care for the members rather than for any organization, and we must be vigilant that no other name be allowed to replace the name of Christ.

God's Care for His People

One day Ahab's eyes fell upon a beautiful vineyard beside

his palace in Jezreel. He said to Naboth, the owner of the vineyard, "Give me your vineyard, that I may have it for a vegetable garden because it is close beside my house, and I will give you a better vineyard than it in its place; if you like, I will give you the price of it in money" (1 Kings 21:2). Ahab was the king, and the richest portions of the country were already his, including many large vineyards. Even his palace in Jezreel was probably not the only one he had. Yet when he saw Naboth's vineyard, all he could think about was that little piece of ground that didn't yet belong to him.

Ahab was obsessed with Naboth's land which was so fertile and ideal for his purposes. He could not tolerate anyone else being so blessed. This happens to many who are in leadership. When we are in charge, though everything is ours, it is easy to become jealous of anyone who is blessed and fruitful. If we are leaders, we want to be the heroes and receive all the glory. To enjoy others' success is difficult for many.

In the church life, we should care for people and raise them up to serve God and stand for His testimony. Every member should be both cared for and caring for others. If we are growing spiritually, it is because we are being cared for by another believer. But are we ourselves caring for anyone? Many of us would have to say no. If we are not taking care of anyone else, we are not yet building up God's testimony. It doesn't matter that we grew up in a marvelous church life, attending first the children's meetings, then the junior high meetings, then the high school meetings, and so on—if we are not caring for others, we are not yet building up God's testimony.

Caring for others cannot be an occasional event. Babies can't be properly raised up by only caring for them once in a while. Children cannot grow up to be healthy if they only have random or intermittent care. The church life is a place of caring for people.

Yet as we labor to raise up others, something peculiar can happen—we become jealous of the successes of those we are shepherding. For example, if we care for high school students, we may unconsciously begin to feel that the high school meeting is our kingdom. Then one day some of them begin to expound the Bible better than we can. This is hard to accept. As those we raised up are recognized and appreciated by others for their ability or fruitfulness, jealousy subtly creeps in. After all, didn't we labor with longsuffering and diligence to help them develop? When the young ones finally begin to mature and become manifest, we may begin to lose sleep over them again, but this time not out of concern for their spiritual growth. Few are willing to raise up others to be their equals, and fewer still are willing to raise up others who will surpass them.

Ahab offered to buy the land from Naboth or even to give him a better vineyard somewhere else. But Naboth replied, "The Lord forbid me that I should give you the inheritance of my fathers" (1 Kings 21:3). When he heard this, Ahab was troubled. He became moody, stayed in bed, and refused to eat. His desire for Naboth's land seems to have driven him to depression.

Ahab was not so evil that he would plot to seize Naboth's vineyard. Jezebel, however, was very evil. When she found out what had happened, she secretly sent letters under Ahab's seal to the elders and nobles of Jezreel to form a conspiracy against Naboth (v. 8). She had them find two worthless men to falsely accuse Naboth of cursing God and the king. Based on this false accusation, Naboth was stoned to death. When Ahab heard that Naboth was dead, he quickly took possession of his land. How evil this was!

As soon as Ahab went to the vineyard to take possession of it, the Lord sent Elijah to proclaim His judgment on Ahab and his family (vv. 16–19). In the past, Elijah might have argued with God and said, "Lord, don't You remember that I fled for forty days and nights to get away from Jezebel? Now You want me to go back bearing news such as this to Ahab. Surely Jezebel will execute me without hesitation. Please send another prophet to do this job. You have shown me that You can use many other prophets. Please send someone else." Elijah's actual response, however, showed his maturity. He realized that even if he were killed, God was able to replace him. Without complaint, he simply followed the word of the Lord. This was no easy decision, but it was necessary to preserve God's testimony by manifesting God's care for His people.

God's Care for His Name

It was after this that Ahab and Jehoshaphat went to war together against the Arameans, even though they had been warned of defeat by the prophet Micaiah (1 Kings 22). After Ahab was killed in battle by the Arameans, his son Ahaziah reigned in his place (v. 51).

One day "Ahaziah fell through the lattice in his upper chamber which was in Samaria, and became ill" (2 Kings 1:2). This illness must have been serious, because he sent messengers to the shrine of Baal-zebub, the god of Ekron, to inquire if his injury would be fatal. This indicates that he was continuing the Baal worship of his father and mother.

Baal means "lord; master; possessor; owner" (Potts, p. 43). When people worship an idol, it eventually dominates them and controls their lives, becoming their lord. There are many "Baals," many different things that can become our lord.

Ahaziah inquired of a certain Baal that he thought could tell his fate. But God cared too much for His name to allow the king of His people to inquire of Baal-zebub. Therefore, the angel of the Lord sent Elijah to intercept the messengers of the king and say to them, "'Is it because there is no God in Israel that you are going to inquire of Baal-zebub, the god of Ekron?' Now therefore thus says the Lord, 'You shall not come down from the bed where you have gone up, but you shall surely die'" (2 Kings 1:3–4).

By sending messengers to an idol, Ahaziah was acting as if there were no God in Israel. Because he denied the name of the Lord, he would die. The Lord, for the sake of His testimony, cannot allow His own name to be replaced by another. God is jealous. No other name should be proclaimed among us besides the name of Jesus, the unique name given to us by God (Phil. 2:9–10).

When Ahaziah's messengers returned, they brought Elijah's message to him. Ahaziah sent out a captain with fifty soldiers to order Elijah to come to him. This captain found Elijah sitting on the top of the hill, and he said to him, "O man of God, the king says, 'Come down!'" (2 Kings 1:9). Elijah answered, "If I am a man of God, let fire come down from heaven and consume you and your fifty" (v. 10). Instantly God sent fire and burned up the king's officer with his men. Then the king sent another captain with another fifty soldiers. Again, they were burned up by fire from heaven. This is hard to understand. Why did these one hundred men and their captains have to die? Didn't Elijah know that these men had families? When Elijah called down fire on these men, he must have created many widows and orphans. This tragedy occurred, however, because the king despised the operation of God by sending soldiers to arrest God's prophet.

Finally, the third captain sent out by the king approached Elijah with humility and respect. Rather than commanding him to come down and stand before the king, this captain humbly bowed down on his knees and begged him to spare his life and the lives of his men. This fearful attitude is appropriate when handling the people and things related to God's government. So Elijah willingly came before the king and repeated the judgment of the Lord he had previously spoken (v. 16).

God judged two consecutive kings of Israel—Ahab and Ahaziah—in order to protect His testimony in relation to His people and His name.

8

Gilgal, Bethel, Jericho, and the Jordan

When Elijah was hiding in the wilderness after fleeing from Jezebel, it seemed as though his service to the Lord was over (1 Kings 19). Even the Lord's next commitment to him included anointing Elisha as his replacement. This seemingly failed prophet then demonstrated great maturity by taking the time to raise up Elisha and train him properly. Additionally, he cared for God's people by dealing with Ahab in the matter of Naboth's vineyard, and he cared for the Lord's name by dealing with Ahaziah for seeking help from a false god rather than from the God of Israel.

Sometime later, "it came about when the Lord was about to take up Elijah by a whirlwind to heaven, that Elijah went with Elisha from Gilgal" (2 Kings 2:1). Through all of his experiences and dealings with the Lord, Elijah was now mature and ready to be taken up, but Elisha still needed additional experiences to become Elijah's replacement.

Both Elijah and Elisha were aware that the Lord was about to take Elijah. Elisha had been with his master for some time, ministering to him, and he probably discerned that Elijah had become different. Elijah must have begun teaching Elisha in a different way, preparing him to serve the Lord on his own. So when Elijah told Elisha to remain at Gilgal while he went to Bethel, Elisha refused. He knew he only had a short time left to learn from Elijah and wanted to make the most of it.

Due to his determination to remain with Elijah, he followed him through four stations before the Lord finally took Elijah. These final four experiences were very precious and were crucial to Elisha's own development as a prophet.

Gilgal—Cutting Off the Flesh

Elijah and Elisha were in Gilgal (2 Kings 2:1). This was where the Israelites first crossed the Jordan into the good land after their exodus from Egypt and where they were circumcised by Joshua (Josh. 5:2–9). Circumcision is a cutting off of the flesh. Therefore, spiritually speaking, circumcised people do not serve God according to their flesh. Today in the churches, there is a great need for us to deal with our flesh. Many of us have attended countless church meetings and conferences. Now we must have the experience of Gilgal, the experience of spiritual circumcision.

Many do not realize how much they rely upon the flesh when they attempt to serve the Lord. Suppose there are three young Christian brothers—one is sweet, one is sober, and the third is very strict. These three come together to decide what the young people in their church should do. The sober brother wants to hold a conference, and the sweet brother says, "Amen." The strict brother wants to have a disciplined training, and again the sweet brother says, "Amen." So the sober brother says, "I have prayed for three days, and the Lord is leading me to have a conference." Then the strict brother says, "I have prayed for four days, and the Lord is leading me to hold a training." The sweet brother says, "I haven't prayed at all, but both are good options. Please don't fight." This kind of "fellowship" is common, but all three are in their flesh, for they serve only according to their fleshly ability. None of them care for what Christ desires, so little actual spiritual service is taking place.

This is why the experience signified by Gilgal is so crucial.

We cannot serve God in our flesh. We must deal with our flesh if we want to follow the resurrected Christ. Our flesh has been crucified (Gal. 5:24; Rom. 6:6). The Lord has nailed it to the cross. Now we are one with Christ (Rom. 6:5) and are resurrected with Him (Eph. 2:5–6). Our flesh has been crucified with Christ. However, most of us still bring our flesh with us into our church life. Often we may think we are being spiritual, when instead we are being fleshly. It is possible to love the Lord yet remain in our flesh. This is why many are not happy in their church life, for they remain in the flesh.

Where did the flesh come from? God formed man out of red clay—Adam means "taken out of red earth" (Farrar, p. 11). Then God breathed the breath of life into his nostrils (Gen. 2:7). This breath of life formed man's spirit within him. When the spirit came together with the body made out of the dust of clay, man became a living soul. God originally intended that man's spirit would be the leading part of his being. He placed man in front of the tree of life so that man would receive God's life. However, Adam ate from the tree of the knowledge of good and evil instead, and thus sin and evil came into man's body (Rom. 7:20–21; 5:12). Immediately, Adam and Eve's condition began to degrade, and because of their sin, all of their descendants also became flesh (Gen. 6:3).

The Flesh and the Self

The fall of man produced two things: the flesh and the self. The flesh is the God-created body with the sinful nature operating within it. We became sinners. We sin because we have a sinful nature. The good part is that we have an active conscience which keeps us sensitive to sin. No matter how sinful people become, their conscience will convict them of their sinfulness. This is why sinners realize that they need God and seek out salvation.

The fall of man also produced the self. The self is especially serious because, unlike sin, it is difficult to detect. It is not necessarily immoral. It is expressed in opinions and viewpoints. Because we have opinions, we often live according to what we think is right rather than according to God.

Immediately after Adam and Eve ate the fruit of the tree of the knowledge of good and evil, they realized they were naked. This was the operation of their conscience. But rather than go to God concerning their nakedness, they sewed together fig leaves to cover themselves (Gen. 3:7). This was due to the operation of the self. Self replaces God, because it makes us think we know what to do. When God came to look for Adam, Adam didn't cry out for help but hid himself. He should have said, "God, please help me. I've messed everything up." Instead, he blamed his wife and even God for his predicament (v. 12). Then Eve blamed the serpent (v. 13). Both of them struggled to cover and protect themselves, and neither was open to God.

The self-life is subtle. It always seeks to defend itself or to amuse itself. The self even amuses itself with the things of God without opening to God Himself. This is why we must pass through Gilgal. You must learn to know our self-life. Otherwise, God cannot use us. If we are not aware of our flesh and self, God will not commit His testimony to us. If we want to serve the Lord with a rich ministry, we must begin with the experience of Gilgal.

Bethel—The House of Salvation

Elijah told Elisha to remain in Gilgal while he went on to Bethel, but Elisha vowed not to leave Elijah. So the two of them traveled together to Bethel (2 Kings 2:2).

Once we begin to have the experience of Gilgal, recognizing that we are fleshly and that we have such a subtle self-life, we need to advance to Bethel. Bethel means "house of God" (Potts, p. 54), and it is the best place to be dealt with and healed. The Lord deals with our flesh and self-life in the house of God, which is the church (1 Tim. 3:15). Not many Christians fully appreciate the value of having a church life. They may enjoy church meetings and admit their value, but few realize that having a church life is a salvation to them.

Once we begin to realize that we have a self-life, we quickly discover that dealing with it is extremely difficult. This is true whether our self-life is timid or aggressive. However, there is one thing we can do, no matter what kind of person we are— we can throw ourselves more and more into the church life.

Every kind of person can be helped at Bethel. We know we have come to Bethel when we begin to experience the church life as our salvation. Whether we are strong or weak, we should love the church. Whether we feel we are gifted or not so gifted, we should love the church. Whether we are sinful, stubborn, or complicated, the church life can be our salvation. If we are organized, diligent, or extremely capable, the church life can also be our salvation. In the church life, we are exposed and our flesh is dealt with, but we are also loved, encouraged, and comforted. It is not always the most comfortable life, but it is by far the most valuable life. Often I tell the Lord, "You are so wonderful. Not only are You my Savior, but You have brought me to a place where I can be saved from my self day by day."

Willing to Pay the Price

While Elijah and Elisha were in Bethel, "the sons of the prophets who were at Bethel came out to Elisha and said to him, 'Do you know that the Lord will take away your master from over you today?' And he said, 'Yes, I know; be still'" (v. 3). These prophets-in-training wanted to show how much they knew, so they boasted of their knowledge regarding Elijah's impending rapture. Yet not even one of them vowed to follow Elijah as Elisha had done. They possessed the same knowledge that Elisha had, but they did nothing about it. When Elisha realized that his master would be raptured, he vowed not to be separated from him so that he might learn something further from Elijah and receive the utmost blessing.

It is interesting that the sons of the prophets referred to Elijah as "your master" rather than "our master." They were content merely to talk about what they knew but had no intention to follow Elijah as Elisha did. This is like many Christians today. They know what is right and proper but never commit to what they know. Are we willing to pay a price to actually follow the Lord, or are we content with knowledge about Him?

The Lord does not reward empty talk. He is looking for those willing to follow Him. It is easy to have some knowledge, but we must eventually pay a price if we want the things we know to become real in our own experience. If we haven't paid the price for the things we know, they aren't really ours at all. This is why Elisha told the sons of the prophets to be still. Although they could talk the talk, none of them were willing to walk the walk.

Jericho—Battling God's Enemy

Elijah said to Elisha, "Please stay here, for the Lord has sent me to Jericho" (2 Kings 2:4). Once again Elisha refused to stay behind and vowed to remain with Elijah to the end. When they came to Jericho, the sons of the prophets who were there came to Elisha and showed off their knowledge in the same way as those in Bethel. Everybody seemed to know that Elijah was going to be raptured, but only Elisha was willing to stay with him and learn from him. How common it is for people to receive knowledge cheaply yet not pay the price to act on what they know. So once again Elisha told them all to be still.

After we come to know our self-life at Gilgal and discover the value of the church life at Bethel, there is still something further—we must go on to Jericho. When the Israelites entered the good land, the first city they conquered was Jericho. After it was destroyed, Joshua prophesied that whoever rebuilt Jericho's foundation would do so at the cost of his firstborn son, and whoever rebuilt its gates would do so at the cost of his youngest son (Josh. 6:26). Therefore, Jericho was a cursed city, and from Joshua's time until Ahab's reign, no one had dared to rebuild it. Yet in Ahab's time, Hiel the Bethelite rebuilt the city with its foundations and gates (1 Kings 16:34). In the process, he lost his oldest and youngest sons, who died according to Joshua's word. Though Jericho should never have been rebuilt, nonetheless it was.

Why would Elijah bring Elisha to such a cursed city? It is because the battle with God's enemy begins at Jericho. Once we know our self-life and appreciate the church life, we must also come to know Satan. At Gilgal, our self-life becomes exposed, and we see how fleshly we are. At Bethel, we find healing and salvation from our flesh and our self-life in the church life. Most of us would be content to remain at Bethel, but the Lord desires to bring us onward to Jericho. The Lord is happy that we see our self-life and that we appreciate His house, but there are also enemies to conquer. We need to go on to Jericho to subdue the authority of darkness.

At Bethel, we are equipped for spiritual warfare. The church life is where we, as the body of Christ, put on the whole armor of God to withstand His enemy (Eph. 6:12–13). As we mature, we should be engaged more and more in spiritual warfare with the spiritual forces of wickedness. At Jericho, we enter this warfare.

The Jordan—Living in Resurrection

After they came to Jericho, Elijah told Elisha once more to stay behind as the Lord called him forward to the Jordan (v. 6). Elisha remained unwilling to leave Elijah. As they went on together, fifty of the prophets-in-training followed at a distance. These fifty were at least better than those at Bethel, who spoke many words but didn't follow Elijah and Elisha. The fifty "stood opposite them at a distance" (v. 7). They were not with the two prophets but were within watching distance. They did not put themselves fully into what was taking place and therefore missed the final words Elisha heard from his master.

After maturing in the church life and entering into the spiritual warfare, we come to the last stage, signified by the Jordan River. At this point, the self is completely terminated, and we are in resurrection. The Jordan is where John baptized Jesus (Matt. 3:13). Our baptism was an experience of the Jordan, and when we were baptized, two things happened: we were buried with Christ, and we resurrected with Him (Rom. 6:4). Our baptism was foundational for our Christian experience.

However, in Elisha's case the Jordan River came at the end instead of the beginning. Why is this? Though new believers taste the experience of resurrection, it is not until we have come to the Jordan after getting to know our self, God's house, and Satan, that we are more able to experience and apply the Lord's death and resurrection.

To become a servant of the Lord who can bear His testimony, we must experience the four stations through which Elisha passed with Elijah. There are no shortcuts. Everyone who wants to serve the Lord must pass through these four stations to experience His full salvation and the power of His resurrection to become His prophet.

9

The Rapture of Elijah

Crossing the Jordan

When Elijah and Elisha came to the Jordan, Elijah folded his mantle and struck the water with it. When he did this, the water parted, and they crossed over on dry land (2 Kings 2:8). Elijah no longer asked Elisha to stay while he went on alone. He knew that this younger prophet would stay with him until the end to glean the last ounce of blessing.

Consider what it must have looked like as they passed through the river together. Once divided, the water must have begun to pile up on one side. By the time they reached the middle of the river, the wall of water must have been quite high. I would have been scared, but they just continued to fellowship as they passed through. Nothing could distract Elisha from hearing Elijah's final words, and Elijah was busy trying to teach Elisha everything he could. What a wonderful relationship!

Requesting a Double Portion

Once they had crossed the Jordan, Elijah told Elisha, "Ask what I shall do for you before I am taken from you" (v. 9). Elijah already knew that God had chosen Elisha to replace him, yet he never displayed any jealousy or hurt pride. Rather, he shepherded and trained Elisha as well as he could. Elijah never saw Elisha as his competition. Instead, he took every chance to pour out all that he had into him. Even at the very end, just before God was ready to take him, Elijah's thought was on what Elisha could receive.

For his part, Elisha knew that one day he would replace Elijah, but he was not wishing that Elijah would depart sooner so he could take his place. On the contrary, he was treasuring every moment with Elijah and receiving everything he could from the older prophet. He honored Elijah as he would honor his father.

If Elijah had asked me what he should do for me, I would have answered, "Dear master, I would like to be faithful to all that you have taught me. You have been a great prophet. Now I am ready to carry on with all the knowledge you have given me." Doesn't that sound like a good answer? However, the more Elisha learned from Elijah, the more he realized that being a prophet is not a matter of knowing doctrine, and the Lord's testimony is not upheld by teaching. He saw that the principle of Elijah's operation as a prophet was a matter of spirit. So he said, "Please, let a double portion of your spirit be upon me" (v. 9).

What a request! He asked not just to have the same spirit as Elijah but to receive a double portion. He asked not just to be as great as his teacher but even greater. The reason Elijah could be such a great prophet was because he had a strong spirit. In everything we pass through with the Lord, having a strong spirit is the true secret.

Elijah must have been shocked by Elisha's answer. Throughout his life as a prophet, Elijah was sometimes bold and at other times frightened, but he was always clear about what he was doing. This time, however, he didn't quite know how to answer Elisha, because such a spirit was not his to give but the Lord's. Elisha was Elijah's most promising student, much more promising than the sons of the prophets who followed them at a distance. But no matter how hard Elijah tried to teach and help Elisha, he could not make him Elijah. So he said, "You have asked a hard thing. Nevertheless, if you see me when I am taken from you, it shall be so for you; but if not, it shall not be so" (v. 10).

Elijah's Rapture

Then, as Elijah and Elisha were walking and talking, a chariot of fire and horses of fire suddenly appeared and separated the two of them (2 Kings 2:10). In the Bible, fire is used to divide and separate. For instance, fallen man was kept out of the garden of Eden by cherubim and a sword of fire (Gen. 3:24). Here, the fire divided the one to be raptured from the one who would remain. Up to this point, I believe Elisha must have been hanging onto Elijah. He was zealous to stay with him, but the fire forced him to let go.

Once they were separated, Elijah was taken up by a whirlwind to heaven. This must have been quite a sight: the whirlwind caught him up and carried him higher and higher until he was gone. One moment Elisha was with Elijah, and the next moment he was alone. As Elijah was being taken up, he let his mantle fall. Even as he was being taken up into heaven, Elijah still was mindful of Elisha and of God's need for a prophet on earth to bear His testimony. It is hard to believe that a man could be that spiritual.

When Elijah was being taken up, Elisha witnessed it. He had been holding on to a great spiritual man, but now his hands were empty and he had nothing. He cried out, "My father, my father, the chariots of Israel and its horsemen!" (2 Kings 2:12). This was truly meaningful.

Firstly, he called Elijah his father, revealing the relationship in life they shared. Elijah was the one who had raised up Elisha in life. In all spiritual things, he was a father to Elisha.

Secondly, he referred to "the chariots of Israel and its horsemen." Elisha saw how God had committed His testimony to Elijah and how Elijah had cared for God's people and fought for His name. With this cry, Elisha was indicating that Elijah was like a horseman safeguarding and directing God's people and testimony. To Elisha's sensation, when Elijah was with them, they were safe and had a way to go on. Now that he was gone, the source of Elisha's life and the one who fought for God's testimony was gone.

Receiving Elijah's Mantle

After Elijah was carried away from his sight, Elisha tore his clothes into two pieces. This tearing of his clothes was a kind of mourning and signified the giving up of the old man (Eph. 4:22–24). Then Elisha picked up Elijah's mantle, which had fallen from him, and he returned and stood by the bank of the Jordan. He struck the water with the mantle as Elijah had done earlier and said, "Where is the Lord, the God of Elijah?" (2 Kings 2:14). He wasn't questioning the Lord's existence. He knew God was there, but he wanted God to confirm that Elijah's commitment had passed to him. He remembered that Elijah had said that receiving a double portion of his spirit was conditional, so he did not yet dare call the Lord, "My God," but instead, "The God of Elijah."

When Elisha struck the water, it parted just as it had for Elijah, and he crossed over. The parting of the water was a confirmation from God that he had received the double portion of Elijah's spirit. When he crossed back over the Jordan, all the sons of the prophets saw him and said, "The spirit of Elijah rests on Elisha" (v. 15). They then came to meet him and honored him.

This was the double portion—on the outside, he was Elijah because he was wearing Elijah's mantle, but on the inside, he was Elisha. If I put my jacket on someone, then from a distance people would think that person was me. But close up, they would discover that it was not me. When the sons of the prophets looked at Elisha, he looked like Elijah, but when they talked to him, it was Elisha. Outwardly, he exhibited the same power and authority as Elijah, but inwardly there was something different.

Speaking Religious Nonsense

Even after such weighty events, the sons of the prophets did not behave soberly. These were the same people who knew Elijah would be taken, but had not dared to put themselves with him. The best of them had only stood opposite at a distance and observed the things taking place. They hadn't followed Elijah closely or held to him tightly as Elisha had. Nevertheless, as soon as Elisha returned, all these junior prophets began to speak total nonsense, saying, "Behold now, there are with your servants fifty strong men, please let them go and search for your master, perhaps the Spirit of the Lord has taken him up and cast him on some mountain or into some valley" (2 Kings 2:16). How foolish this was! Elijah had just been caught up into heaven, but they wanted to search for him in the mountains and valleys.

Why did they want to search for Elijah when they knew he had been taken by God? It appears they wanted to involve themselves in what had happened, even though there was no more possibility. To search for Elijah was useless, but momentarily it made them seem important. Elisha told them there was no need to search for Elijah, but they continued to talk about this until it became a big issue. By making an issue out of such nonsense, eventually they frustrated Elisha and made him feel ashamed (v. 17). Maybe they accused him of not caring about Elijah. They may have begun to slander him, suggesting that he was so pleased with being Elijah's replacement that he didn't care about looking for him.

Finally, he told them to go and search. Of course, they couldn't find him—everybody knew that he had been raptured. Those who had murmured against Elisha for not sending them to search may also have murmured against him for sending them on such a fruitless three-day mission. Perhaps the word began to spread that Elisha had no faith, because he wanted to search for Elijah when everyone knew that he had been raptured by God. Such things can happen.

Even among those dedicated to the Lord's testimony, some will want to say or do something to show how important they are. Like the sons of the prophets, they generate useless issues and produce conflicts over nothing. I love Bethel, the church as the house of God, but I hate religion. Religious people have too many opinions. Regardless of what others do, it will be wrong in the eyes of religious people. When others do something, they will say they are fleshly, but if others do nothing, they will say they are lazy. When people are in the realm of self-importance rather than in the realm of Christ, they become foolish and create issues. They are like the sons of the prophets in Elisha's day, manifesting the self in their speaking. If we do not want to become such people, we must be like Elisha, living according to the spirit and standing for the testimony of the Lord.

Elijah was the greatest prophet in the Old Testament according to the principle of God's power. Elisha was covered with this power outwardly, but inwardly he operated according to the principle of God's divine attributes expressed through human virtues. This is why Elisha never calls down fire or holds back the rain. Rather, the humanity expressed through him corresponds to the principle of the New Testament.

10

Elisha's
Operation (1)

Two Prophets, Two Principles

The way God operated in the Old Testament age differs from the way He operates in the New Testament age. In the Old Testament age, He operated by means of His power and authority. He still uses His power and authority in the New Testament age, but in a way that manifests and dispenses Himself as life. The New Testament principle is that God dispenses His divine life into us, regenerating and reconstituting us into sons of God, enabling us to produce and carry out what God desires.

Elijah is the prophet who most characterizes the Old Testament principle. In the New Testament, he represents all of the Old Testament prophets. For instance, when he and Moses appeared together with Jesus at His transfiguration (Matt. 17:3), Moses represented the law, and Elijah represented the prophets.

Elijah always operated according to the principle of God's power. He was so powerful that no one could stand against him. He shut up the heavens so that no rain could fall. He slaughtered all the prophets of Baal. These were demonstrations of God's power. Then, twice when Ahaziah the king sent fifty men to order Elijah to come to him, Elijah called down fire on them. This indicated that the true authority did not rest with the king but with God. Through Elijah's works of power, God demonstrated His authority. Elisha, on the contrary, prefigured God's New Testament principle by operating through the dispensing of life. Elisha wore Elijah's mantle, so he likewise had God's power and authority. With both Elijah and Elisha, there was termination and death, but with Elisha, there is also life germination and resurrection. Here was a man with all the power and authority given by God to Elijah. However, his name was not "Jehovah is God" (Strong, no. 452) like Elijah but "God is salvation" (Davis, p. 216). With Elijah, it was clear that Jehovah was God, but He could still be separate from man. With Elisha, this same powerful God was intimately involved with man to save him in every situation. Elijah was burdened for God's testimony and had primarily sought to have the people recognize Jehovah as their God and repent from their idolatry. Elisha was also burdened for God's testimony, but the way he cared for it was by dealing with its substance and content. Therefore, wherever he went, he set things right and put things in order.

These two prophets go together. All that Elijah represented and passed through eventually led to Elisha. They even traveled together through Gilgal, Bethel, Jericho, and the Jordan. Elijah's ascent in the whirlwind introduced Elisha to God's people, for when Elijah was raptured, Elisha became manifest to Israel as God's blessing to His people as Elijah's continuation.

Two Sections of Elisha's Ministry

Elisha's ministry can be divided into two sections. In the first section, his operation was in the principle of the resurrected humanity of Jesus Christ. This means that Elisha displayed not a natural humanity, but the fine humanity of Jesus Christ. This humanity passed through many different experiences and was constituted with all the divine attributes. This stage of Elisha's ministry focused on meeting man's need.

In the second section of Elisha's ministry, his operation was with divine authority in resurrection. In this stage, his ministry focused on accomplishing God's desire.

The remaining chapters of this book cover fifteen stories and incidents from Elisha's ministry. The first five stories display the resurrected humanity of Christ, and the last ten stories portray the divine authority of resurrection in the church life (five stories) and in the kingdom life (five stories).

Jericho—Healing the Water

Once Elijah was taken up, Elisha returned from the Jordan River to Jericho, retracing the steps through which he had passed with Elijah, and began to operate as God's prophet.

When he arrived at Jericho, the men of the city told him, "Behold now, the situation of this city is pleasant, as my lord sees; but the water is bad and the land is unfruitful" (2 Kings 2:19). Since Jericho was close to the border between the kingdoms of Judah and Israel, it was strategically located. It also may have been beautiful. The problem was that the land was barren because the water was bad.

The first thing Elisha did when he came to serve God's people in the principle of the humanity of Christ was to heal the water. We should not think that our spiritual environment plays only a minor part in our growth. Let me use my education as an example. When I entered high school, I was ten years old and the youngest student in my class, but by the time I graduated, I was twenty years old. Why did it take me ten years to complete four grades? In my sophomore year, the Communists overran the city we were living in, so my family had to flee to another city. When we arrived there, I restarted my sophomore year. After about a semester, the Communists came to that city as well, and once more we had to flee. When we came to the third city, I began my second year for the third time. The same thing happened twice more. I attended five different schools, yet in none of them was I able to complete my sophomore year. I was in a poor environment for academic growth. It was nearly impossible to learn under such circumstances. After my family finally arrived in Taiwan, however, the entire situation changed. In addition to having a stable school environment, I also received the Lord. My ability as a student suddenly blossomed. This illustrates why Elisha began by first healing the water of Jericho. Without a healthy environment, it is hard to experience the proper growth in life.

Elisha asked the men of Jericho to bring a new jar with some salt in it (v. 20). A new jar symbolizes that the old way does not work anymore (Mark 2:22). The vessel must be made new. Sometimes after people are revived at a conference, they go back to their local church with the intention to start a revolution. We should always submit to the leaders of the church and appreciate those serving among us (1 Thess. 5:12–13). What we can do, however, is exercise our new life in the Spirit to produce a new jar. Our church life will be made fresh because of us. It will become vital, cohesive, operative, and filled with brotherly love. Our church life must become a new jar, a new vessel. We don't need to itemize everything we think is wrong with our church. What is needed is a new jar. If we would supply our church with the divine life, it will become a new vessel.

Elisha asked that salt be put in the new jar. Salt is a preservative. Salting meat preserves it because salt kills germs and other infecting elements. Salt also makes things tasty. A little salt added to bland food makes it flavorful. When I was a teenager, I had a kidney sickness, and the doctors said I could not eat salt for a year. This seems like a small thing, but the whole quality of my life changed. I began to lose my appetite, because all my food lacked flavor. In the process of producing a new jar in our local church, we shouldn't rebuke the leaders. That isn't salt; that's jalapeno pepper! We should learn to become salty. The new jar must have salt in it.

In Jericho, everything seemed good, but in fact, something was wrong, and this affected everything. Today in our church life, we may have high truths and revelation, but something may be missing. The test is, are we fruitful? Do we have a harvest? Are the new believers among us growing properly? Elisha's response to the situation in Jericho was to throw salt from a new jar into the water. The salt out of the new jar healed the water so that it no longer caused barrenness. With this miracle, Elisha healed the environment that was frustrating the proper growth.

Bethel—Mocking Elisha's Baldness

After healing the waters at Jericho, Elisha continued on to Bethel. As he approached Bethel, some boys came out from the city and began mocking him saying, "Go up, you baldhead; go up, you baldhead!" (2 Kings 2:23). Elisha then looked at them and cursed them in the name of the Lord. Two female bears came out of the woods and killed forty-two of these young boys.

It was only when Elisha came to Bethel, which means "house of God" (Potts, p. 54), that we find out that he was bald. Up until this time, neither Elijah nor the sons of the prophets had pointed this out. The church life, today's house of God, is the most exposing life. No matter how well we are growing and serving, the church life will expose our limitations. In the church life, we are all baldheads. The more we are together in the church life, the more we see one another's baldness. This is why the leadership in another church appears wonderful and spiritual, while that in ours seems deficient.

The church life is exposing, and no matter how spiritual we may be, we are still imperfect human beings. There is always a temptation to exalt a spiritual man. Martin Luther's disciples desired to exalt Luther. John Nelson Darby's disciples desired to exalt Darby. However, we must realize that every human being, no matter how spiritual, is a baldhead. Even the apostle Paul admitted that he had weaknesses (2 Cor. 12:9). However, we should not point out or talk about the weaknesses of others.

When I was young, I thought that all the church elders and all those serving me were perfect. But as I grew, I began to see that none of them were angels. When this happens, it becomes tempting to say to them, "Go up, you baldhead! Get out of here!" I have received help and care from many. Gradually I realized that all of them had their limitations. I never criticized them nor spoke about their weaknesses and limitations because I recognized that they were the Lord's servants. This is one of the greatest blessings I have received from the Lord.

When I was a college student, I spent a year in a certain city in Taiwan. One day as an elder passed by, I thought I smelled cigarette smoke. Smoking is a habit that is almost impossible to hide. Smokers may think they are careful, but in the end everyone will know. After a few similar incidents, I realized that this elder smoked. In other words, I saw his bald head. By the Lord's mercy, however, I never said a word to anyone, but instead I prayed. Two or three weeks later, he gave a testimony in which he said, "You do not know the power of sin; you even have no way to overcome a little three-inch cigarette." When he said that, I thanked the Lord, for his testimony indicated to me that he had been healed by the Lord.

What if, instead of praying privately, I had laid this matter before the young people I was serving and asked them all to pray for this brother? That was a small church, so everyone would soon have been talking about this. If I had asked the whole church to pray for him, would that have been a blessing or a curse to the church? Would it have helped or frustrated that elder? Everyone may have prayed fervently, but whenever they saw him, they would have thought, "Oh, the smoking brother is here." In the church life we are all bald, but it is not our business to criticize, point out, or make an issue of the baldness of others, especially of those who serve us.

Elisha looked at the young mockers and cursed them in the name of the Lord. Two female bears then came out of the woods and killed forty-two of them. This reveals how grave a matter it is to touch those who serve God and represent His authority. Touching God's authority in an improper way will cause our spiritual life to suffer drastically. Mocking and personal criticism have consequences, even when disguised as caring fellowship. We should always avoid the habit of criticizing those who serve us. If we have this habit, we need a deep repentance, or it will become nearly impossible for us to go on with the Lord.

Elisha was different from Elijah. Elijah might have just called down fire from heaven and burned them all up, as he did with those sent to bring him to the king. But Elisha did not do anything directly. He didn't command the bears to attack the young people. He simply left the matter in the Lord's hands and continued on his way. It was God who decided that the mocking had gone too far.

How serious it is to criticize those who serve and lead us in the church! Even when their weaknesses become known to us, we shouldn't criticize them, or our spiritual life before the Lord will be affected. Let us learn to respect the elders and those who serve us. They give their lives to the Lord, to the church, and to us and are a life supply given by God. Do they have shortcomings and failures? Yes. Are they limited? Yes. But these are not matters for us to talk about.

Getting Involved with Three Kings

The next story of Elisha is easier to understand than the previous two. The previous two were related to growth, but this story is related to function. How we function as members of the body is always easier to understand than how we grow in life.

Jehoram the king of Israel became angry with Mesha the king of Moab because Mesha refused to pay the tribute he had previously paid to Jehoram's father, Ahab (2 Kings 3:4–5). So Jehoram gathered Jehoshaphat the king of Judah to him as well as the king of Edom. These three went up together with their armies against Moab. Three kings should have been able to easily defeat one king, but before they even reached Moab, they got into trouble, for they ran out of water.

None of the kings had thought to consult a prophet in order to hear what the Lord had to say about their venture. Their motives had been purely political. It wasn't until they ran out of water that Jehoshaphat finally asked whether there was a prophet available so that they could ask the Lord for help. A servant of the king of Israel replied, "Elisha the son of Shaphat is here, who used to pour water on the hands of Elijah" (v. 11). So the three kings went to see this prophet who had been so close to Elijah and had ministered to him.

Elisha received them in an interesting manner. If three kings visited any of us, we would probably be flattered and would treat them honorably. Elisha, however, spoke roughly with Jehoram, saying, "What do I have to do with you? Go to the prophets of your father and to the prophets of your mother" (v. 13). By this, he meant the false prophets who served idols. He never even addressed or acknowledged the king of Edom. The only king he showed any regard for was Jehoshaphat the king of Judah. Elisha said, "As the Lord of hosts lives, before whom I stand, were it not that I regard the presence of Jehoshaphat the king of Judah, I would not look at you nor see you" (v. 14).

I like Elisha's response to these prominent men. Elisha was learning that once people become manifested servants of God, many will come to seek their advice. However, a servant of the Lord cannot afford to become a mere problem-solver.

Elisha wouldn't even have given them the time of day had it not been for Jehoshaphat.

Elisha asked for a minstrel to play some music for him (v. 15). Elisha had never previously needed a musician. Because this request was outside the scope of his ministry, he needed help to be inspired to prophesy.

A Valley Full of Trenches

Elisha told them, "Thus says the Lord, 'Make this valley full of trenches....You shall not see wind nor shall you see rain; yet that valley shall be filled with water, so that you shall drink, both you and your cattle and your beasts'" (2 Kings 3:16–17). So they filled the valley with trenches, and in the morning the trenches were filled with water for the soldiers and animals to drink.

When the Moabites looked into the valley, the sun's reflection made the water in the trenches look like blood. They mistakenly thought that the three kings had fought among themselves, so they rushed down to take the spoils. To their surprise, the Israelites rose up and struck them. Thus Elisha's work of power was doubly effective—it provided water for the Israelites and their allies, and it became the source of defeat to their enemies.

After winning this battle, the Israelites began to ravage the land of Moab. As they marched through, they covered the fields with stones, cut down the good trees, and stopped up the springs according to the word of the Lord spoken by Elisha (vv. 19, 25). When they arrived at the fortified city of Kir-hareseth, the king of Moab grew desperate. He went out onto the wall and sacrificed his oldest son, the heir to his throne, as a burnt offering.

The result of all this was that "there came great wrath against Israel, and they departed from him and returned to their own land" (v. 27). What a strange end to this story!

Even after the miracle of water in the trenches took place according to Elisha's word, the Israelites did not accomplish what they set out to do. Elisha seemed to be useful, but in the end nothing came out of his involvement. There was great anger against Israel, and everyone just went home.

Staying within God's Measure

This story warns us against getting involved with what God has not apportioned to us. Elisha became involved in something that did not concern him, and the help he rendered the three kings because of his regard for Jehoshaphat was a waste of lives, time, and resources as far as God's testimony was concerned.

We should not become busybodies in our church life. Some things have not been measured to us, but it is tempting to get involved anyway. I am able to minister the word, but I am not very effective at giving gospel messages. Sometimes I am invited to a place to give a gospel message, but I always tell those who invite me that gospel preaching is not my portion. If they insist, I may come and dig some trenches to be filled with water. Everyone will be refreshed and have their thirst quenched, but few will be saved. Such a gospel message will not have much long-term result for the establishment of God's kingdom since it is beyond what the Lord has apportioned to me.

It is healthy to desire to take every opportunity to serve. We love the Lord, so if a gospel message needs to be preached, we should be available. If someone is needed to visit new believers, we should be available. If there is a need for some to serve the young people, we should make ourselves available. If someone is needed to mow the lawn, we are available. When we serve with the humanity of Jesus, on the one hand, we should make ourselves available to everyone and to everything, but on the other hand, we should also consider what the Lord has committed to us. We won't grow and develop well if we are too easily persuaded to help with every campaign that comes along.

When we try to operate outside of what the Lord has committed to us, the best we can do is dig some ditches. When they fill up with water, everyone may be refreshed, but in the end, the result will be disappointing, because we have gone beyond what the Lord has committed to us. It is a difficult lesson to learn that we do not need to be busily involved in every matter, but we must be faithful to what the Lord has committed to us.

God uses this story to tell us not to become busybodies, regardless of how others may seek after us, for it will not result in a meaningful furtherance of the Lord's testimony. The miracle of the water filling the trenches was wonderful, but in the end it accomplished nothing. Israel won a battle, but Moab was not subdued. By this we should realize that, regardless of how talented or capable we are, we should serve God within our measure and according to His leading rather than going beyond what He has apportioned to us.

The Jar of Oil and Borrowed Vessels

The fourth story, which concerns a poor widow, once again shows Elisha operating in the principle of the resurrected humanity of Christ. This widow had been the wife of one of the sons of the prophets. She cried out to Elisha, saying, "Your servant my husband is dead, and you know that your servant feared the Lord; and the creditor has come to take my two children to be his slaves" (2 Kings 4:1). This was a pitiful situation.

Elisha asked her, "What shall I do for you? Tell me, what do you have in the house?" (v. 2). All she had was a jar of oil. So he told her, "Go, borrow vessels at large for yourself from all your neighbors, even empty vessels; do not get a few. And you shall go in and shut the door behind you and your sons, and pour out into all these vessels, and you shall set aside what is full" (vv. 3–4). She and her sons obediently borrowed as many vessels as they could and gathered them all into her house. Then she shut the door and began to pour oil from her jar into the borrowed vessels. The oil from that one little jar filled all the vessels they had borrowed. The widow kept pouring the oil without stopping until the last vessel was filled, at which point the oil stopped. Then Elisha told her, "Go, sell the oil and pay your debt, and you and your sons can live on the rest" (v. 7).

This widow had depended on her husband. When she lost him, she didn't know what to do. In our church life, we may rely upon someone who is like a spiritual mother or father to us, who helps us care for our spiritual children. One day, however, this spiritual parent moves away. Suddenly our support is gone, but those around us must still be cared for. Then "the creditor"—the devil—comes to take our spiritual children to make them slaves to the world. This difficult situation may occur again and again in our Christian experience.

In a sense, Satan, God's enemy, has a legal claim, but in another sense his claim is illegal. He is legal, because God gave him a certain measure of authority on the earth, but any claim he has is illegal, because he rebelled against God. God still uses Satan. He is wrong and evil, but God has allowed him some room to run around and cause trouble. He works as an evil creditor to try to snatch away our spiritual children at the exact moment we lose our support. As soon as our spiritual parent is gone, those we care for start to get caught in worldly things. We feel like the poor widow fearing her children will become slaves to the creditor and wondering where to turn for help.

When this widow came to him, Elisha didn't ask her how much money she needed and then pay off her debt. Instead, he asked her, "What do you have in the house?" All she had was one jar of oil.

This jar of oil represents Christ as the life-giving Spirit (1 Cor. 15:45; 2 Cor. 3:17). What we have is nothing but the Lord Jesus Christ. Our only possession is the Spirit in our spirit (Rom. 8:10–11). Even if we have no ability, no experience, no wisdom, and no truth, we have our spirit, and in our spirit is a very rich Christ.

The widow and her sons borrowed vessels from their neighbors. For us, this means we must go and borrow many vessels to contain all the riches of the Spirit in our spirit. We must find others into whom we can pour our burden for our spiritual children. We should pour what we have into others as we fellowship and pray with them. They are not our vessels, but we can borrow them. The more vessels we gather, the more the oil flowing out of our spirit will be multiplied. No matter what situations we face throughout our entire Christian life, we will always have our jar of oil. And as long as we have our spirit, we can draw strength from the body of Christ by pouring out from our spirit into the many vessels.

It was a laborious process for the widow to fill all those vessels. Oil is thick and heavy, so it poured slowly and caused her arms to grow tired. One of her sons may have helped to hold her arms while the other brought vessel after vessel to be filled. Yet out of this exhausting effort, so much blessing was produced. The more the oil is multiplied, the greater the blessing.

When I speak at conferences, I pour oil into the spirits of those who attend. For me to give a series of messages is tiring, but I must pour what oil I have from my jar, because there are many empty vessels waiting to be filled. If no one came, the oil would stop.

What a wonderful possession is the Spirit in our spirit! Those who serve the Lord should never be in need. If we become "widows," we need to remember that we still have a jar of wonderful oil. It is not true that some have high quality oil and that others have poor, thin oil. We all have the same Spirit within our spirit. As long as we follow the Lord, this oil will never run out. It is the source that will carry us through every difficulty.

The Woman from Shunem

The last incident showing Elisha operating in the principle of the resurrected humanity of Christ involves a woman from Shunem. This story has two sections. The first part (2 Kings 4:8–17), which is covered here, concerns this woman's care for Elisha and culminates in the prophet healing her barrenness. The second part, which will be covered in the next chapter, involves the child whom the Lord gave her through Elisha's promise (vv. 18–37).

Shunem was a town near Jezreel. Elisha often traveled in this area. As he passed through Shunem, he was invited to eat a good meal in the home of a prominent woman there. He became a frequent guest in that household, enjoying that woman's hospitality. After some time, the woman said to her husband, "Behold now, I perceive that this is a holy man of God passing by us continually. Please, let us make a little walled upper chamber and let us set a bed for him there, and a table and a chair and a lampstand; and it shall be, when he comes to us, that he can turn in there" (vv. 9–10). The room they prepared for him, with all its items, shows how considerate they were in providing for the needs of the Lord's servant.

Elisha appreciated her care, so he asked what he could do for her. Not only was Elisha a prophet of the Lord, but he also knew the king and the commander of the army (v. 13). If she had made any request, he could have obtained it for her. The woman simply replied, "I live among my own people" (v. 13). Her reply indicated how pure she was. Her taking care of Elisha was not for any reward or favor but because she and her husband cared about him and loved him as a servant of God.

Few are this simple or pure. If the Lord Jesus were to ask us what He could do for us, we might ask for an upgrade in our standard of living, a promotion in our career, or success in our education. We are full of asking and seeking. Even if we dare not say so, our heart constantly desires something.

How pure this woman's reply to Elisha was! She simply stated that she was content to live among her people. She did not even mention that she and her husband had no children. It was Elisha's servant Gehazi who pointed this out. Once Elisha heard this, he told her she would be holding a son in her arms by the same time the following year. The woman's response to Elisha's promise was, "No, my lord, O man of God, do not lie to your maidservant" (v. 16). I don't believe she spoke in this way because she lacked faith. She was simply saying, "Elisha, I am content as I am. What you promise is almost more than I could have hoped for, but if you say you will do it, then please fulfill your word." In the following year, she indeed brought forth a son according to his word (v. 17).

We all have to thank the Lord. He provides for the environment of the church life with a new jar filled with salt. In this environment, even if our baldness is exposed, it doesn't matter, because here young believers grow to maturity, and there is no criticism but rather love and the covering of one another's weaknesses, failures, and limitations. In addition, we should not run around as busybodies. Instead, we should be restricted to what the Lord has measured to us and be content to labor faithfully within this boundary. Furthermore, we should never forget that we have a wonderful Spirit in our spirit that can be poured into all the vessels around us, thus becoming a rich source of blessing. In this way, we will be pure and able to bear fruit in the church life.

11

Elisha's
Operation (2)

Operating in the Church Life

Elisha's name means "God is salvation" (Davis, p. 216), and his operation conveys the principles and experiences of God becoming our salvation. The first five stories of his ministry, as seen in the previous chapter, portray the resurrected humanity of Christ. The last ten stories portray the divine authority of resurrection in the church life and the kingdom life. The five stories concerning the church life will be covered in this chapter, and the five concerning the kingdom life will be in the next.

The Death of the Shunammite's Son

In the first of these five stories, the son of the woman from Shunem was born to a family who loved the Lord. As he grew up, he probably became proud, having been born as the result of the promise of the man of God. One day, he went out to the field where his father and the reapers were working. After he got there, he began to moan, "My head, my head" (2 Kings 4:19).

Today, those who are born into a family that loves the Lord can also become proud, because they are continually told how special they are. They walk among everyone planting and watering in God's New Testament field, the church (1 Cor. 3:6–9), just like the son walked among the workers in the field. As they listen to so many glorious testimonies and good messages, they get so stuffed full of doctrines, teachings, and knowledge that their heads hurt, yet they have so little experience of Christ. This story should warn us that in the organic church life, knowledge alone does not work. Nothing that is merely inherited or based on knowledge can be used for the building up of the organic body of Christ. The only things that build up are the riches of Christ which have become ours through experience.

Young believers don't need so much knowledge. They will be more blessed if we simply help them to love the Lord, live in the Lord's presence, and love the Bible. We should help them touch Christ and nurture their trust in God's governmental arrangement. None of these matters require extensive knowledge.

When the boy began to complain about his head, his father sent him home. Fortunately, this boy had a good mother. As soon as she saw him, she sat him on her lap and tried to comfort him. She could do nothing for him, however, and sadly, he died. Immediately, she laid him on the prophet's bed and rode off as fast as she could to find Elisha.

When she found the prophet, her conduct was remarkable. Instead of pouring out her anguish, she initially said nothing, but fell down and held on to Elisha's feet. Elisha's attendant Gehazi didn't like what she was doing and tried to push her away. This is what happens when those who serve lack the ability to interpret what is really going on. Elisha had to tell him, "Let her alone, for her soul is troubled within her; and the Lord has hidden it from me and has not told me" (2 Kings 4:27). Although the Lord had not revealed it to him, Elisha knew that something serious must have happened.

Then the mother prayed a good prayer. She said, "Did I ask for a son from my lord? Did I not say, 'Do not deceive me'?"

(v. 28). She was reminding Elisha that he had promised that she would have a son, and she put all the responsibility on him. We should learn to pray to God like this. He has made so many promises to us in His Word. We need to remind Him that He is responsible to fulfill them in our experience.

The Resurrection of the Shunammite's Son

As the woman of Shunem spoke in this way, Elisha must have immediately realized what had happened. He handed his staff to Gehazi and told him to go and lay it on the boy's face. Elisha's staff signified his authority. Therefore, he was in effect telling his attendant to go in his authority and power to resurrect the boy. Gehazi went, probably feeling proud and excited about such a commission, and laid the staff on the boy's face. However, nothing happened. I don't believe he returned right away to report this to Elisha. He probably tried many ways to resurrect the boy because he wanted to do it himself. He had seen his master work many miracles, and he had possibly heard Elisha speak on such things. He may have tried to lay the staff on the boy's face from different angles. He may have shouted, "Wake up! In the name of the Lord, wake up!" Eventually, he had to report to Elisha, "The lad has not awakened" (2 Kings 4:31).

Many Christians are like Gehazi. They enjoy carrying the staff of authority more than they care for those they serve. When Gehazi went to resurrect the boy, I doubt he even prayed, because he was so preoccupied with his big chance to work a miracle. Elisha told him not to greet or talk to those on the way (v. 29). This would have given him time to pray for the boy throughout the entire trip. Had Gehazi prayed all the way to Shunem, his heart surely would have been full of feeling and care for the child. Instead of caring for the dead boy, however, he only cared for the staff of authority that was now in his hands. All that Elisha cared about was the dead child, but all of Gehazi's attention was on the staff. Gehazi probably tried hard to resurrect the boy, but eventually what works is not what we are told to do, but who we are. We shouldn't be Gehazis. We must learn to love those we serve more than our service. We must care for them with a spiritual commitment, not as an assignment or an opportunity to exercise authority.

The Lord would not use Gehazi. He borrowed Elisha's staff and tried to use Elisha's way, but in serving the Lord, nothing that we borrow from others works. Only what has become ours is effective. Perhaps the woman sensed this, because she didn't race ahead with Gehazi, but remained with Elisha.

When Elisha reached the house, he entered the room, shut the door, and prayed to the Lord. He stretched himself out on the boy, putting his mouth on the boy's mouth, his eyes on the boy's eyes, and his hands on the boy's hands. As he did this, the boy's flesh became warm. Elisha got up, walked around a little, and then stretched himself over the boy again. At this point, the boy sneezed seven times and opened his eyes. Elisha told Gehazi to call the boy's mother.

The way Elisha raised this boy from the dead was different from the way Elijah raised the widow's boy (1 Kings 17:17–24). What Elijah did was entirely a matter of power. He called out strongly to the Lord and then lay on the widow's son three times. With Elisha, however, it was not merely a matter of power—the staff itself was not enough. Rather, he exercised the resurrected humanity to dispense the resurrection life and power into the boy. This is signified by his putting "his mouth on his mouth and his eyes on his eyes and his hands on his hands" (v. 34).

Would we have been willing to do such a thing to a dead person? It probably took at least one day for the woman to find the prophet and then for him to return to her house. By then, the corpse was cold. However, Elisha did not shy away from this awful death; he cared so much for this dead boy. The source of death is sin, and sin is mainly related to what we say, what we see, and what we do. Elisha came to bring life to this boy. Therefore, he put his living mouth on the dead mouth, he put his living eyes on the dead eyes, and he put his living hands on the dead hands.

When those who have grown up in the church life experience the resurrection life of Christ, they begin to speak living words, see heavenly things, and serve in a life-giving manner. This is the experience of resurrection in the church life.

After Elisha stretched himself upon him again, the boy sneezed seven times, sneezing out all the elements of death completely. Sneezing is a sign of sickness. The fact that the boy sneezed seven times signifies that he completely sneezed out all the death-inducing germs.

The church life is composed of those who have experienced the power of resurrection. In the church life are many frustrations, causes of stumbling, and even the presence of death itself, but if we know the power of resurrection, such things shouldn't trouble us. Are we willing to put ourselves right into someone else's situation of death? Can we care for weaker ones so closely that we are mouth to mouth, eye to eye, and hand to hand with them? If we love them to this extent, they will surely be able to receive life from us and be revived.

Elisha's raising the boy from the dead demonstrates the first principle of the church life—it must be in resurrection. The more we are in resurrection, the more we will become a blessing to the church.

Neutralizing the Poison in the Pot

The second story began after Elisha raised the Shunammite woman's son from the dead and returned to Gilgal (2 Kings 4:38). There was a famine in the land, yet remarkably, Elisha did nothing to end it. He simply allowed the sons of the prophets to gather around him.

We may wonder why he didn't pray in a powerful way for rain and for the famine to end. We do not like to see the church life experience famine. We want everything to be promising, encouraging, and prevailing with the supply of the Spirit continuously gushing forth. Sometimes, however, there is a shortage of life supply in the church life. When the environment was terrible, rather than ending the famine or fixing the situation, Elisha's way was to simply let others live in his presence.

Elisha said to his servant, "Put on the large pot and boil stew for the sons of the prophets" (v. 38). Even in famine, the Lord is faithful to provide us with something to eat. We may not get steak every day, but as we follow the Lord, something will be provided.

One of the sons of the prophets went into the field to gather herbs. He found some wild gourds and cut these up into the stew, making it poisonous.

The apostle Paul said, "When you assemble, each one has a psalm, has a teaching, has a revelation, has a tongue, has an interpretation" (1 Cor. 14:26). Whenever we come together to meet, it is as if we are all bringing whatever we have to make a big, spiritual pot of stew. Everyone brings various herbs and other ingredients, but someone may also bring something that is poisonous. Once in a meeting, someone declared that the Chinese were God's chosen race, and that the garden of Eden was located in China. His speaking was like poison added to the pot.

The son of the prophet who introduced the poison was not evil. For instance, a Christian salesman may truly believe that the product he sells will benefit everyone who buys it, so he may promote it every time he meets other believers. Eventually, however, when he looks at them, he no longer sees Christ but potential customers. His church life thus becomes poisoned because he brought in something other than Christ.

Elisha dealt with the poison in the stew simply by throwing

some meal into the stew. The meal represents the high and fine humanity of Christ. When Elisha put the meal into the stew, it neutralized the poison.

Suppose a believer I know comes up to me walking in a disoriented way. I soon realize that he has been drinking alcohol. What should I do? If I were to say, "You drunkard, get away from me," then I would probably drive him away. Instead, I should exercise a high humanity. I might say, "Dear brother, what has happened to you?" He might respond, "Oh, I am fine. I just came from the bar. Hallelujah. Amen." So I take him to my home, give him some food, and put him to bed. In the morning, he may wonder where he is. I shouldn't greet him by saying, "You were going straight to hell, but I rescued you!" If this were my manner, I would lose him after rescuing him. So I say, "Brother, last night I saw you wandering around. I brought you here so you wouldn't get hurt. Did you sleep well? Let me make some eggs for you. How would you like them cooked? Do you like white or wheat toast?" After such care, he will have no choice but to love the Lord. Over time, his poison will be healed through the fine humanity of the resurrected Jesus Christ.

Too often we become lawgivers and tell others what they have done wrong. A healthy church life is not filled with judgment but with the exercise of the humanity of Christ to restore one another (Gal. 6:1). We need those who love and show mercy toward one another with a high humanity (1 John 4:7). Such a church life will be filled with restorations. If some bring in poison, we love them and heal them with the humanity of Jesus.

It is different if someone poisons others intentionally. If someone is deliberately attempting to damage others, the church leaders should protect the congregation (Acts 20:28). However, this son of the prophets was just a naive person who had no intention of bringing in poison. We should labor to restore such ones.

The Barley Loaves

Immediately after the poisonous stew was healed, a man came from Baal-shalishah with twenty loaves of barley and fresh ears of grain as bread of the first fruits (2 Kings 4:42). This third story goes together with the previous one.

The famine at Gilgal exposes the situation among Christians today. During a time of seeming shortage, some who are naive may let their self life poison their church life. Therefore, we must exercise to heal and restore them with the high humanity of Christ, neutralizing their poison so that neither they nor others are damaged. Out of this kind of exercise, the church life will become very life-giving—suddenly there will be an abundance of spiritual food. Our exercise of the high humanity of Christ produces an abundance of resurrection in freshness, signified by barley, the first crop to ripen in the good land.

The man from Baal-shalishah gave the loaves to Elisha's attendant, but the attendant said, "What, will I set this before a hundred men?" (v. 43). The man told him, "Give them to the people that they may eat, for thus says the Lord, 'They shall eat and have some left over'" (v. 43). And it happened just as the Lord said.

One hundred people ate those loaves and were satisfied. This represents a full and satisfying experience. When there are some who possess such a fine humanity, the need in the church life will be satisfied, no matter how many people there are. It is not a small thing to meet the need of the church with the humanity of Christ. How we need the Lord's mercy so that we may be a church filled with the humanity of Jesus in resurrection! If this is our case, many barley loaves will be produced to meet the need of all those who are blessed to be with us.

Curing the Leprosy of Naaman

The fourth story involves Naaman, who was a great and

highly respected leader of the Aramean army (2 Kings 5:1–
14). However, this great man was a leper. Leprosy is a disease
that sometimes is hidden and sometimes is apparent on the
skin. In Elisha's day, it was incurable. However, a slave-girl
from Israel told Naaman's wife, "I wish that my master were
with the prophet who is in Samaria! Then he would cure him
of his leprosy" (v. 3). Based on her word, the king of Aram
sent Naaman to Israel with a letter for the king of Israel. He
took servants, horses, and chariots, and he brought ten tal-
ents of silver, six thousand shekels of gold, and ten changes of
clothes as gifts. The letter from the king of Aram to the king
of Israel seemed to demand the impossible, so the king of
Israel began to worry, saying, "Am I God, to kill and to make
alive, that this man is sending word to me to cure a man of
his leprosy? But consider now, and see how he is seeking a
quarrel against me" (v. 7). Just then, Elisha sent word to send
Naaman to him.

Eventually, Naaman and his entourage arrived at the house
of Elisha. We can imagine the scene as General Naaman rode
up with all his servants, chariots, and horses heavily laden
with the gold, silver, and fine garments. When he was an-
nounced, however, he was not ceremoniously received. Elisha
did not even come out to see him. Instead, he sent a messenger who merely opened the door and said, "Go and wash in
the Jordan seven times, and your flesh will be restored to you
and you will be clean" (v. 10).

Naaman became indignant when he heard this. He was
used to being treated honorably, and Elisha's lack of respect
must have seemed insulting. What's more, he was told to
travel to the Jordan and wash seven times in its waters. He
may have thought that Elisha was mocking him, so he said,
"Are not Abanah and Pharpar, the rivers of Damascus, better
than all the waters of Israel? Could I not wash in them and be
clean?" (v. 12). As Naaman turned to leave in a rage, his servant reasoned with him, saying, "My father, had the prophet
told you to do some great thing, would you not have done it?

How much more then, when he says to you, 'Wash, and be clean'?" (v. 13). Because of his servant's wise word, he went and dipped himself in the Jordan seven times. As he did so, his flesh was restored like that of a little child. This is a picture of the Lord coming to save us from our inward sin. We all are plagued with the leprosy of sin. When it is not visible, others may appreciate us as being so good, but the Lord sees how sinful we are. No matter how good we are reputed to be, the leprosy of sin is present with us. Even after we have been buried and resurrected in baptism, we should not allow sin to reign in our mortal bodies, so that we obey its lusts (Rom. 6:12). We must be exercised concerning our flesh throughout our entire life. No matter how long we have loved the Lord, we should always be aware that inwardly we have an element that is very ugly. We must exercise self control in our church life and not give the leprosy in our flesh an opportunity to develop. By not giving the flesh any opportunity to be expressed, we shall become clean and godly.

Too often, however, we are eager to show off our leprosy to one another. For instance, a meek, young Christian sister may find it difficult to testify in a home meeting. One day, however, the Lord may provide her something quite rich to speak. Afterward, everyone is impressed, but none may realize that inwardly she feels proud to be able to speak better than others.

We need to go down into the Jordan not just once but seven times. How easily we can become a source of leprosy in the church life yet feel we are fine! Sometimes the Lord seems to have no way to deal with us. If He doesn't give us any encouragement, we feel hopeless, yet if He gives us a little success, it can rouse the leprous element of sin within us. It is risky for the Lord to allow us any success, because as soon as others begin to appreciate us, we begin to think we are the angel Gabriel or the next Moses. When we feel that we have accomplished something or that we have something, at that moment we must wash ourselves again in the Jordan.

Otherwise, we will become a problem in the church life. We must constantly deny sin the opportunity to rise up and reign within us.

The Borrowed Axe

We now come to the last of the stories portraying divine authority of resurrection in the church life. The sons of the prophets felt that their place had become too limited. Perhaps many prophets had joined them, and they had increased in number. Therefore they said, "Please let us go to the Jordan and each of us take from there a beam, and let us make a place there for ourselves where we may live" (2 Kings 6:2).

I like this principle of each one bringing one beam for the enlargement of the building. If everyone in a church could gain one new convert every year, that church would double annually.

As all the sons of the prophets were working hard to cut down trees to use as beams, one of them got into trouble. While he was swinging his axe, the iron head flew off into the water. He cried out, "Alas, my master! For it was borrowed" (v. 5).

This indicates again that nothing borrowed is good for building up the church. If we use something borrowed, it is going to become ineffectual. In the church life, we may borrow a good message or some truth from others. In the short run, we may be able to provide beams to build up the church, but eventually our borrowed axe head will lose its effectiveness. We may hear someone pray a spiritual prayer, but if we borrow it by trying to pray the same prayer, it will fall flat. Everything in the church life must be real and genuine. In a school, teachers may teach with knowledge that they borrow from others, but we must pay a price to acquire Christ ourselves if we wish to build up the church. In the world of business or education, people may steal ideas from others, but in the church life, every word we say must belong to us. Every testimony we give must be our genuine experience. In building up the church, what is most effective is our own experience of Christ. This doesn't mean that we shouldn't learn from others or imitate the older believers, but we lay hold of the real things for ourselves. Whatever we borrow from others must become ours before it can be useful for building.

Elisha cut a stick and threw it into the water. This caused the axe head to float so that young prophet could pick it up for himself (vv. 5–6).

That stick signifies the cross of Christ and the floating axe head portrays resurrection. Everything we have borrowed—all the truths we have been taught and all the wonderful spiritual advice we have received—must pass through the cross and enter resurrection. Until we begin to know the cross and experience resurrection, our labor cannot be effective in building up the church. As we learn to take the cross, all the knowledge we have borrowed will become experiential and will bear the divine authority of resurrection.

These five stories of Elisha portray a wonderful progression in our experience of the church life. First, the raising of the Shunammite's boy indicated that the church life is fully in resurrection. Death is conquered in the genuine church life. Yet even though we are in resurrection, we still encounter difficulties, indicated by the famine in Gilgal. Nevertheless, the Lord will always provide food for us. And just as the poisoned stew was healed with meal, we can heal unhealthy situations in our church life by exercising the fine humanity of Jesus. Through such an exercise, we will bring forth many barley loaves to abundantly supply those in need. However, the story of Naaman reminds us that we are still lepers. We must keep ourselves in the death of Christ. Moreover, the story of the borrowed axe tells us that our participation in the church life must be completely genuine. What we use to build up the church must be the Christ that we ourselves have laid hold of and made our own. What we pick up from the ministry of others must become ours. We must gain something of ourselves so that the church may be enlarged through our labor.

12

Elisha's Operation (3)

Fighting for God's Kingdom

The previous two chapters cover ten stories concerning Elisha's operation in his ministry, typifying a person living in resurrection with Christ's humanity and laboring for God's testimony, the church. This chapter covers the last five stories, which portray the kingdom in the way of experience, not doctrine. The first five stories produce a begetting person. The next five produce a person with a genuine function in the church life, ready to live a life of fighting for God's kingdom, because the kingdom life is a fighting life.

The Aramean Army's First Invasion

In the first incident regarding fighting for God's kingdom, the king of Aram was waging war against Israel (2 Kings 6:8–23). Previously Israel had waged war against Moab, but now Israel was being attacked by the Arameans. Jacob himself was an Aramean (Deut. 26:5), so Israel was being attacked by relatives. When we are young, our enemies are those on the outside, unbelievers, but as we mature, those who persecute us are those near to us, those we love.

As the Aramean king maneuvered to attack Israel, he found that the Israelites always knew what he was planning and frustrated his attacks. He became enraged because he assumed that Israel had a spy among his servants who was passing on his plans to Israel. Then one of them told him, "Elisha, the prophet who is in Israel, tells the king of Israel the words that you speak in your bedroom" (v. 12). When the Aramean king realized that even his most hidden plans were known to Elisha, he decided he must capture him. Therefore, he sent a massive army to surround the city of Dothan, where Elisha was dwelling. The more we become effective in fighting for God's kingdom, the more the enemy will use everything at his disposal to neutralize us.

When Elisha's attendant saw the Aramean army surrounding them, he became terrified. Elisha told him, "Do not fear, for those who are with us are more than those who are with them" (v. 16). We all should memorize this verse! Then Elisha asked the Lord to open his attendant's eyes to see that the hills around them were filled with heavenly, fiery chariots.

When the Arameans came down to Elisha, he asked that God would strike them with blindness. In spiritual warfare, God often blinds our enemies. Elisha then took charge of the blinded Aramean army and led them to the king of Israel in Samaria. The Israelites easily could have slaughtered them all, but Elisha had the king of Israel serve them a good meal instead. Afterward, the Arameans returned to their king and no longer bothered Israel.

The first principle of spiritual fighting is that when people persecute us, the Lord will blind them and even put them in our power. We must learn to treat our enemies well and show them love (Rom. 12:20; Luke 6:27). People, particularly those in the religious realm, tend to despise those they see as enemies. Those who live in resurrection, however, manifest love toward all.

The Aramean Army's Second Invasion

The second story shows that even this will not solve all the problems. In spite of our kindness toward them, people may still attack us. After Elisha graciously sent the Aramean soldiers home, their king attacked Israel with an army, besieging the city of Samaria (2 Kings 6:24–7:20). The famine within the city grew so severe that a donkey's head was sold for eighty shekels of silver, and dove's dung was sold for five shekels of silver (2 Kings 6:25). In this time of extreme famine, even useless things became expensive. It was difficult for God's people to find a way to survive.

When spiritual famine strikes, many ask the Lord, "Why are You allowing this to happen?" Although they struggle to produce a harvest, the Lord doesn't allow it. In 1942, Watchman Nee was excommunicated by the church in Shanghai. He did not attend any church meetings during this time, so he must have experienced spiritual famine. The church in Shanghai also experienced famine and disbanded shortly thereafter. This was the work of God's enemy fighting against the church of God. When spiritual combat comes, the Lord allows frustration, persecution, and famine to come upon us in extreme measure.

A woman came to make a complaint to the king of Israel (v. 28). She and another woman had made an agreement to eat their sons for their own survival. The first day, this woman boiled her son, and they ate him. But the next day, the other woman hid her son.

I like that the woman wouldn't allow her son to be eaten, but wouldn't it have been even better to let her son eat her? This is the heart of true servants of the Lord—they never sacrifice the younger ones for their own survival.

This story shook Jehoram the king of Israel. When he heard it, he became angry at Elisha and at God, vowing, "May God do so to me and more also, if the head of Elisha the son of

Shaphat remains on him today" (v. 31). This vow echoes the one made by Jezebel to kill Elijah (1 Kings 19:2). Eventually, the king went even further, saying, "Behold, this evil is from the Lord; why should I wait for the Lord any longer?" (2 Kings 6:33). Besides vowing to kill God's servant, he accused God Himself.

We may think we trust in the Lord, but then hardships come. We feel surrounded and suffer an inward spiritual famine. We may cry out, "Why should I wait for the Lord any longer? Why should I continue to follow Him? It is so meaningless." The Lord will continually try us, not until we become victorious, but until we are completely defeated.

It was not until the king of Israel expressed his complete defeat by blaming Elisha and God that Elisha prophesied that the famine would be lifted the next day. Fine flour and barley would then be sold for next to nothing (2 Kings 7:1).

The Lord defeated Israel's enemy once more: "The Lord had caused the army of the Arameans to hear a sound of chariots and a sound of horses, even the sound of a great army" (v. 6). There was no great army to defeat the Arameans. They only heard what sounded like a great army and fled in terror, leaving everything behind in their camp. Not only were they defeated, but all their food supply and equipment became available to the Israelites. The famine was lifted in one day, just as Elisha had prophesied. It is only after we have been so completely defeated that the famine will be lifted and the enemy will flee.

Sojourning among the Philistines

The third story once more involves the woman from Shunem who begot a son according to the promise of Elisha and whose son was later resurrected by him. After the two invasions by the Arameans, Elisha came to warn her that the Lord had called for a famine upon the land for seven years (2 Kings 8:1).

After the first invasion, the Israelites treated their Aramean enemies to a nice meal. After the second invasion, the Aramean enemies fled too quickly to enjoy their hospitality but were good enough to leave all their food and riches behind. The third disaster, however, was a seven-year famine ordained by the Lord.

At times, it seems as though God is the author of disaster. As we follow the Lord, there will be times when one disaster follows another. No matter how disastrous our life may be, by the Lord's mercy, we can still give glory to God. To fight for the Lord is to enter into the most difficult and yet most glorious kind of life.

Elisha's warning to this woman is hard to understand. He told her, "Arise and go with your household, and sojourn wherever you can sojourn" (v. 1). She ended up leaving the good land and dwelling in the land of the Philistines for those seven years. Why should God's people run away to live among the Philistines? It would have seemed better if they had fled to Judah, which was part of the good land. When I was young, I never understood why Martin Luther accepted so much help from Frederick III, Elector of Saxony. Yet this story of the Shunammite woman indicates that at times God does use the Gentiles to protect His people.

Submitting to the Lord's Choice

Through one disaster after another, it became clear that God was in control of everything. Therefore, after the seven-year famine, Elisha traveled right into Damascus in Aram, the place from which the enemies had been attacking (2 Kings 8:7). The Aramean king, Ben-hadad, was sick and dying. When he heard that Elisha was in Aram, he sent Hazael to inquire of the Lord by Elisha whether he would recover from his sickness. When Hazael did so, Elisha told him, "Go, say to him, 'You will surely recover,' but the Lord has shown me that he will certainly die" (2 Kings 8:10). The next verse is powerful: "He fixed his gaze steadily on him until he was ashamed, and the man of God wept" (v. 11). Elisha wept because he knew the evil that Hazael would do to God's people. God had told Elijah to anoint Hazael as king over Aram (1 Kings 19:15). Now, around thirty years later, Elisha essentially fulfilled this commission by telling Hazael, "The Lord has shown me that you will be king over Aram" (2 Kings 8:13). If it were up to Elisha, he would never anoint a king who would eventually slaughter so many Israelites.

Even though Elisha knew that Hazael would damage Israel and bring great harm to God's people, he was faithful to do what God required of him. I might have been tempted to say, "Lord, if You want to set this evil man as king over Aram, then please find another prophet to do it." However, having passed through all these phases of spiritual combat, Elisha realized that the Lord knew exactly what He was doing. Even during times of intense persecution and suffering, the Lord is still the Lord of all. Although Elisha wept as he foresaw the evils that Hazael would commit, he still trusted that God was all-knowing and all-wise. He knew that the Lord was appointing a king who would become a persecutor of God's people, yet he submitted to the Lord's choice.

Jehu Anointed King

After Hazael became king of Aram, Elisha had Jehu anointed king over Israel (2 Kings 9:1–11). This completed the fulfillment of every part of the commitment God had given to Elijah (1 Kings 19:15–16). We see not only God's government and choice in making Jehu king, but also His judgment in telling him to strike the house of Ahab. God chose Jehu to avenge the blood of all His people and prophets who had been slaughtered by Jezebel.

Once he was anointed, Jehu moved swiftly. He rallied the army around him and drove furiously to Jezreel, where Jezebel dwelt. Messengers came to ask his intentions, wanting to know whether there would be peace, but he didn't give an answer. In short order, he killed Ahab's son Joram, who was still the king of Israel, and Ahaziah the king of Judah (2 Kings 9:14–28). Next, Jehu dealt with the wicked Jezebel. Her own servants threw her down from an upper window, and she was trampled underfoot by Jehu (vv. 30–37). Then the dogs ate her, fulfilling Elijah's prophecy (1 Kings 21:23).

Even after this, the judgment of God did not lighten. Jehu wrote a letter to the guardians of the seventy sons of Ahab, saying, "Select the best and fittest of your master's sons, and set him on his father's throne, and fight for your master's house" (2 Kings 10:3). The guardians of Ahab's sons realized that none of the seventy had the ability to withstand Jehu. So they answered, "We are your servants, all that you say to us we will do, we will not make any man king; do what is good in your sight" (v. 5). Jehu ordered them to behead all of Ahab's sons, utterly wiping out Ahab's family. Then, after all this, he slaughtered the worshippers of Baal and destroyed their temple, making it a public restroom. "Thus Jehu eradicated Baal out of Israel" (v. 28).

Although he was brutal, Jehu accomplished everything that the Lord had commanded him to do, executing His judgment. He was the king who finally did away with the worship of Baal in Israel.

Afterward, he should have said, "Hallelujah! Let us go down to Jerusalem to worship the Lord our God with our brothers in Judah at the appointed times." However, once a man has control, it is hard for him to let go. Like Jeroboam before him, he realized his kingship would have been threatened if he led his people back to Jerusalem to worship God at His temple. Therefore, he allowed the people to continue worshipping the golden calves in Dan and Bethel. He avenged all the sins of Ahab's family, but he did not depart from the sins of Jeroboam (v. 29).

This shows us how power seduces. When we have control or influence over any part of God's work, it is easy to hold onto it as our own. Thus, because of his grasping self-life, Jehu cannot be counted among the few kings who were completely faithful to what God desired.

Striking the Ground with Arrows

During this time, Israel met defeat after defeat at the hands of Hazael, king of Aram. After all this fighting, Elisha became mortally ill. Joash, the king of Israel at that time, went down to Elisha and mourned over him, saying, "My father, my father, the chariots of Israel and its horsemen!" (2 Kings 13:14). This was exactly what Elisha had cried when Elijah was taken up in the whirlwind (2:12). The king was upset because he knew that the nation would be unprotected once Elisha died.

Elisha had the king bring a bow and some arrows and told him to shoot an arrow toward the east, in the direction of Aram. He put his hands over the hands of the king while the king shot the arrow. Elisha said, "The Lord's arrow of victory, even the arrow of victory over Aram; for you will defeat the Arameans at Aphek until you have destroyed them" (13:17).

Then Elisha told the king to strike the ground with the rest of the arrows. The king struck the ground with the arrows three times and stopped. Elisha became angry with him, saying, "You should have struck five or six times, then you would have struck Aram until you would have destroyed it. But now you shall strike Aram only three times" (v. 19). Elisha never told the king what striking the ground meant, nor how many times to strike it. Nevertheless, he became angry with the king for only striking the ground three times. He had always been such a sweet prophet. His humanity had always been fine and gracious. At the very end of his life, almost with his last breath, Elisha became angry because this was such a sober matter, so closely related to God's desire.

Striking the ground with the arrows was related to victory in the land. In the first chapter of this book, we saw that God's focus has been on gaining the land and gaining a man to work on and rule over this land, even from the beginning in Genesis. Now we see a man striking the land with arrows to bring in God's victory.

Joash was able to bring in victory because "Elisha laid his hands on the king's hands" (2 Kings 13:16). When Joash shot the arrow toward Aram, in the eyes of God the victory over Aram was won. Why then did he have to strike the ground with the arrows? It was because God's focus was not on Aram but on the land. If today we completely defeat one enemy, tomorrow another enemy will attack. The focus of victory is not the defeat of enemies but the gaining of the land. Even if we overcome one problem or difficulty, others are ready to take its place. We must possess the land.

God has given us local churches today as our land. These churches are so precious because they are related to God's man on the land. How wonderful it is that there are some today who care about this land! In so many local churches, many are striking their arrows, fighting to possess the land.

To be a servant of the Lord is to care about the land. No matter how good or mature we are as God's servants, if we are not related to a local church, our function and usefulness before God are up in the air. Therefore, we are blessed if we have some land we can strike with our arrows. In other words, we are blessed to have a local church to labor in, to build up, and to fight for. If we are merely good, promising Christian workers, we may find ourselves serving an institution rather than serving the Lord in our local church. If we serve an institution, though we may serve many people, we are not serving the land. This is the difference between those who serve the Lord for His testimony and those who serve an institution. In our Christian life, we can be busy with many spiritual things, but if our labor is apart from a local church, the result will not be satisfying to the Lord. Our life is to serve the Lord in the land.

Striking to the Full Extent

The arrows that Joash struck the ground with typify the gifts that the Lord has given us. Joash only struck the ground three times rather than the five or six times that Elisha wanted. This shows that we must fully develop whatever the Lord has given us. We may think that the victory is already in hand simply because the Lord has given us some gifts as arrows. It is too easy to be lazy, to strike the ground with our arrows a few times and then quit. Many times I am sorrowful in spirit, for I observe so many gifted, promising believers who are lazy in pursuing the Lord, lazy in spending time in His presence, lazy in their consecration, and lazy in their spiritual exercise. They may strike the land, but never to the full extent.

To hit the ground only three times means we feel our current level of consecration is adequate. We think we have offered ourselves to the Lord enough, labored enough, and sufficiently submitted ourselves to Him. No, it can never be enough! Everything else can be overdone, but we can never give too much or go too far in loving the Lord.

Love the Lord! Love Him diligently with your whole being! Don't be like that foolish, half-hearted king of Israel. Victory was in his hands, but he would not lay hold of it. Tell the Lord, "I would like to be Your servant. I desire nothing but Christ. My life is for nothing but Christ. I am not here to strike at the ground for You half-heartedly. I will strike to the full extent with the arrows You have given to me. I will strike and strike until You have Your victory and testimony."

Death and Victory

Victory did not come until Elisha died. After his death, Joash defeated Aram three times and retook the cities of Israel which had been captured by Hazael, king of Aram (2 Kings 13:20–25).

The Lord is able to bring us through trials, sufferings, persecutions, and disasters. By means of this process, we are brought on to maturity. Once we are mature, we are able to protect those around us from all that threatens. We must fight to become mature so that we may be useful servants of the Lord in local churches, even raising up church after church. It is glorious to live a life for God's testimony on the earth. Such a life holds the highest value, even in eternity.

Works Cited

Davis, John D. *Davis Dictionary of the Bible.* Nashville, TN: Royal Publishers, Inc., 1973.

Farrar, John. *The Proper Names of the Bible.* London: John Mason, 1855.

Hitchcock, Roswell D. *New and Complete Analysis of the Holy Bible.* 1869.

Nee, Watchman. *Twelve Baskets Full, Vol. 2.* Kowloon, Hong Kong: Hong Kong Church Book Room Ltd., 1971.

Potts, Cyrus A. *Dictionary of Bible Proper Names.* New York: The Abingdon Press, 1922.

Strong, James. *A Concise Dictionary of the Words in the Hebrew Bible.* Madison, NJ, 1890.

Online Ministry by Titus Chu

MinistryMessages.org is the online archive for the ministry of Titus Chu. This includes audio messages, articles, and books in PDF format, all of which are available as free downloads.

FellowshipJournal.org is an online magazine that features recent sharing by Titus Chu. It also provides brief, daily excerpts from his ministry, as well as news of upcoming events.

"Daily Words for the Christian Life" is an e-letter sent out every Thursday. It features selections from the writings of Titus Chu. To subscribe, visit FellowshipJournal.org/subscribe.

Books by Titus Chu

The books listed below are available in print, Kindle, or iBook format. To purchase them, go to MinistryMessages.org/order. They are also available on Amazon.com and iTunes.

David: After God's Heart

Elijah & Elisha: Living for God's Testimony

Ruth: Growth unto Maturity

Philippians: That I May Gain Christ

A Sketch of Genesis

Two Manners of Life

www.ingramcontent.com/pod-product-compliance
Lightning Source LLC
Chambersburg PA
CBHW031624040426
42452CB00007B/659